Autonomy and Mercy

Reflections on Mozart's Operas

Ivan Nagel

TRANSLATED BY MARION FABER
AND IVAN NAGEL

Harvard University Press
Cambridge, Massachusetts
London, England
1991

First published as *Autonomie und Gnade: Über Mozarts Opern,*
© 1988 Carl Hanser Verlag München Wien.

This book is printed on acid-free paper, and its binding materials have
been chosen for strength and durability.

Design by Annamarie McMahon

Library of Congress Cataloging-in-Publication Data
Nagel, Ivan, 1931–
[Autonomie und Gnade. English]
Autonomy and mercy : reflections on Mozart's operas / Ivan Nagel ;
translated by Marion Faber and Ivan Nagel.
p. cm.
Translation of: Autonomie und Gnade.
ISBN 0-674-05477-6 (acid-free)
1. Mozart, Wolfgang Amadeus, 1756–1791. Operas. 2. Opera.
I. Title.
ML410.M9N1313 1991
782.1′092—dc20
90-22827

Contents

Mercy and Autonomy: An Essay

Pamina's Three Deaths; or, the Happy Ending

Mercy and Autonomy: An Essay

☾

The Decline of the Sovereign

... resterà ben poco
Dello spazio infinito,
Che frapposer gli Dei fra Sesto e Tito.

Metastasio

I

All expression in opera seria derives from the two gestures
of menace and entreaty. Their alternate pleas fill its song
with pain-kindled eloquence; moreover it was the very
fervor and pathos of their strife that had first urged music
into speech, speech into music, thus founding the genre.
Menace and entreaty (Monteverdi's *Ira* and *Supplicatione*)
are not mere episodes in the action of the serious genre, but
the source of its form. That is why opera in its early history, still nervously unsure of its right to exist, clung to the
story of Orpheus. The wrathful one will hear the prayer of
his supplicant only when he is singing. In a world ruled by
devastating supreme willfulness, opera, rapt in sorrow and
obsessed with lament, is needed to advance a claim for
mercy. – For the next hundred and eighty years, the fables
in music, like their expressive modes, proceeded from a
fateful curse or judgment through lamentation to gracious
appeasement. From ancient tragedy, the composer learned
that same lesson (unless he forgot it in Armida's magical
gardens): to translate a relation of power into a duration of
dialogue, and then to freeze the movement of dialogue in a
tableau of mercy *(katharsis)*. This is how Gluck was still
using his Baroque-bowdlerized Aristotle. The overture to

Iphigénie en Aulide moves within "a single contrast," between a motif that "strides onward relentlessly" and another that "suffers tenderly" (Wagner); it seizes "the grand idea of Greek tragedy by filling us with terror and pity *in alternation*," that is, cast in two parts. – The menacing, terrorizing one is called god or monarch; the entreating, suffering one, man as subordinate. Opera seria is the genre of absolutism. It knows autonomy only as sovereignty, the privilege of the One.

Two Mozart operas in the serious genre are being performed ever more frequently these days. *Idomeneo* and *La clemenza di Tito* have broken into the repertory with the help of a few directors and conductors of integrity, who loathed the exclusionary pact between cowardly management and lazy audiences at the big opera houses. Once upon a time restricting the repertory to masterpieces allowed the canon to shine forth (from behind heaps of historical treasures amassed by the bourgeoisie) as the chalice of innermost meaning in a high culture. Today, their stubborn repetition apes the listening habits of pop fans, who love anything as long as they've heard it often enough. – As to "masterpieces," the culture industry and the media have replaced the act of cognition with the reflex of mindless recognition. But they wash away even the chance for "unknown masterpieces" to reach our ears and brains by flooding us with merchandise of new-old titles. The sudden proliferation of *Idomeneo* and *La clemenza di Tito* in audio and video makes it no easier to discern whether they belong in, fall outside of, or explode a canon than did their long absence from the repertory. What may a canon of operas hold today, and what can it mean? The answer cannot be modeled on the current multiplicity of supply and simple-mindedness of consumption—nor can the question be warded off by mending the rotten fences of the old repertory. The criterion of what is to endure can be sought only in the genre's own law of change.

An odor of absurdity has always clung to that artform in which "people must sing ariettas and dance around graves when a city is destroyed" (Voltaire). Nor could the popular success of its practice cover up the gap in plausibility of its theory, as long as the idea of imitation controlled European aesthetics. In such distress, opera acquired a singular power: each of its major works has the task and the gift of justifying the genre anew from the ground up. It is not only the tangible splendor of their details that irradiates *Le nozze di Figaro* or *Tristan,* but the evidence that a new site in the human soul has been found from which song soars of necessity. To have joined, through sheer sound, all emotion, speech, and action into a new kind of interdependence is what distinguishes, despite their structural weaknesses, *Boris Godunov* from *Die Meistersinger* and, forty years later, *Pelléas et Mélisande* from *Salome.* These works that went on writing the history of man as subject stand out from the unwieldy corpus of all operas as the better, nonhierarchical canon. – The paradox that opera recognizes only the inimitable as the exemplary drove scholars to a methodological divide: producing either sympathetic exegeses of masterworks or a dry, historicist listing of types. The idea of the canon as an assembly of unrepeatable models degenerated in the popular guides to the opera.

The seven operas from the last decade of Mozart's life, which succeeded in breathing subtly nuanced life into the human form, each in a different, unexampled-exemplary way, demand the canonical view. Questioning the content and consistency of *Idomeneo* and *La clemenza di Tito*—the Mozartean seria—serves here to introduce another question. Is there a guiding idea in Mozart's operas that pierces the typology of seria, singspiel, buffa and illuminates each work in turn as a canonic creation—as an unrepeatable moment in the awakening of man as subject? Such an idea would have to circumscribe that place at which the sovereignty of the One is supplanted by the freedom of the individual. Mercy and autonomy separate, contend, suffuse each other there: two eras, two political doctrines, two ontologies.

2

If the action of the serious genre drives onward from the judgment to the final appeasement of a divine/princely wrath, then *clemenza,* mercy from above, must stand as reliably at the end of opera seria as marriage does at the end of opera buffa. This means that the serious genre always unfolds between two estates, the comic genre always within a single estate, mankind. Mozart's *Figaro* and *Tito* seem to disprove the tenet, each in a contrary way: the buffa this time is based on differences of estate, and the seria on the concept of mankind. In *Figaro,* the paradox is solved by a stroke of genius: it is precisely that thorn of genre-contrariness which spurs the genre to its purest triumph. When Mozart slipped an intrigue of inequality into his ensemble opera, whose sweetly interwoven voices never stop anticipating the last finale of equality among free men— then he was endowing each situation with an abundance of obstacles and dangers, but the whole with an unstoppable drive toward the telos of reconciliation. Only beyond all strife about station and privilege, amid the final recompense, are the *dramatis personae* permitted to come to a halt. They do not each clutch their own good fortunes, but celebrate reverently, a chorus beyond division, the beckoning fulfillment: "Ah, tutti contenti *saremo* così!" All happiness will be ours.

The paradox of *La clemenza di Tito* is different. Into the libretto for a pure recitative-and-aria opera that Metastasio wrote in 1734, Mozart (when he set it to music after almost sixty years and forty other composers) set eight ensembles; Tito sings in no fewer than three of them. The emperor takes a part among parts to justify himself, indeed to excuse himself, as a human among humans. By renouncing "divini onori" in his very first recitative, he surrenders the godlike essence of a prince. The space of the seria, its range of expression between the one who menaces and the one who entreats, is thus destroyed. How could fear or hope cry and struggle for mercy, when Tito, a tenorially stiff, pale plaster cast of Sarastro, keeps on declaring that he is no "monster and tyrant," but "a man"? Each incident is debilitated by the shriveling of conflict, and the whole by loss of aim when, from the opening measures, the emperor is praised as most kind and merciful— by the rebel who schemes to kill him. De Sanctis, the Risorgimento republican, mocked the prearranged barter of largesse at the end, which in the late seria, reducing all dangers to sham, invariably brings glory to the prince and promotion to the conspirators: "Tutti eroi e tutti contenti." All of them heroes, all of them happy.

If the buffa *Le nozze di Figaro* was urged forward by the presumption of inequality among the essentially equal, so the seria *La clemenza di Tito* could be motivated by the striving for equality among the essentially unequal: conspiracy. The republican complot against the monarchy provided the plot for one of the great political plays of post-antiquity, the model for Metastasio's libretto, apparently hardly altered: Corneille's *Cinna*. Its first edition in 1641 bore the subtitle *La clémence d'Auguste*. Augustus appears after his bloody conquest of the throne, that is, at the end of civil war. His sovereignty—any unlimited sovereignty—justifies itself precisely as the rule which puts an end to "les fureurs d'une guerre civile": a rule legitimate until the people forget what they suffered, and did, in the war of everyone against everyone. *Cinna* was written soon after the religious massacres, amid the brawls of the high aristocracy, which Richelieu ruthlessly put down. Thus Corneille knew to what extent absolute dominion was evil and necessary.

This Metastasio and Mozart no longer knew. They let a conspiracy of apolitical people peter out in an act of mercy void of politics.

3

The conflict of *Cinna* is not political simply by virtue of the great disputation between the monarchy and the republic which towers at its center. In contrast to Metastasio's Vitellia, vacillating grotesquely in her private rancor, Corneille's Emilie, the daughter of a father slain by Auguste, firmly embodies and propels the conspiratorial action, because, for her, being republican means being an avenger. Retribution begets retribution in civil war; with each day and each deed, ever more inescapably, the web of vengeance becomes the web of the world. Princely mercy cuts through it as an analogue to divine miracle, achieving the inconceivable: one party of the civil war is abruptly transformed into the whole of a peaceful state. The pardoned conspirator kneels and herself undergoes a transformation, four tenses in two adamant lines: "Ma haine va mourir, que j'ai cru immortelle; / Elle est morte, et ce coeur devient sujet fidèle."* – Mercy is a voluntary self-limitation, and hence the proof, of omnipotence. By repealing the lawful verdict of that omnipotence, mercy—amnesty—declares

---

*My hatred, which I thought was immortal, shall die; / It has died, and this heart becomes a loyal subject.

an end to civil war. By the same feat, it separates the sovereign from the tyrant (or the revolutionary dictator), who remains chained to the unending labor of rooting out each of his opponents.

Just as the ghost of bloody civil war still lurks in every corridor, behind each arras of the imperial palace, so the tyrant keeps shadowing the sovereign. Seneca was the first to tell the tale of the generosity of Augustus, in his treatise *De clementia*—which he dedicated to Nero. The sovereign is nothing without power and inclination to tyranny; they constitute one of his godlike attributes. The man who does not fear God does not believe in him. The Dear God was first invented in the age of incipient atheism, the Dear Prince on the way to the French Revolution. Both, if they existed, would be characterized by renunciation. Surely in Corneille too, the emperor's mind is tempted to renounce the throne, while his soul is assailed by melancholy. Not even in his entrance tirade, boastful with heady supremacy, can the splendor of his dominion chase away the specter of old murders: *rang* is glued to its rhyme, *sang*. "Cet empire absolu sur la terre et sur l'onde, / Ce pouvoir souverain que j'ai sur tout le monde, / Cette grandeur sans borne et cet illustre rang, / Qui m'a jadis coûté tant de peine et de sang . . ."* But such gloom remains a political complaint: its anamnesis is complicity in the suicide of a people; its cure, founding the new state.

Metastasio's flattering portrait of the sovereign, on the other hand, allows a ruler no choice but to abdicate into mere humanity. The court poet, a virtuoso of submissiveness, helped the absolute regime convince itself that it was legitimated by the personal kindness of the prince, not by

*This absolute rule over land and sea, / This sovereign power I exert over the entire world, / This unlimited grandeur and illustrious rank / That have cost me so much suffering and blood . . .

the political hatred among the citizens. After ninety years, the *Cinna* material could become suitable again for the court (unbloodied and bloodless) only through its de-

politicization into the private sphere. Tito scowls and forgives his unfaithful friend instead of the traitorous subordinate: "Viva l'amico, benchè infedele!" His temptation to renounce the throne shrinks to the mechanical habit, limp with homoerotic grief, of renouncing love, which he sullenly practices on Berenice, Servilia, Vitellia. Even mercy feels like a habit turned into constraint, not liberation to something new, when he timorously tears up the death sentence: "Ah, non si lasci il *solito* cammin." Don't leave the usual path! The predictability of Tito's character conceals a repetition compulsion, stamped out by a twofold pressure: first, to prove his private self-control (which incessantly undercuts his public power), and second, to exhibit his political mercy (which keeps sapping his inmost self-assertion). – It is precisely as a private person that the disabled ruler seeks refuge in ceremony: in the theatrical device of *clemenza,* which no longer functions to establish the absolute state, but instead every night, with laudatory fanfares and choruses in a sumptuously torchlit finale, bears the state to its grave.

4

In 1791, Mozart's opera for the coronation of Leopold II once more cites the Baroque cosmos of power, only to seal its falling apart into privacy and representation. While *La clemenza di Tito* reduces the prince's emancipation and levels him into the ensemble, it tries at the same time to distinguish audibly Tito's dignity and wisdom from Sesto and Vitellia's passionate mêlées, from Annio and Servilia's childish idyll. Yet against the animated sopranos of three women and one castrato, the strained tenor has the effect of being not a man and sovereign, but the true castrato. Tenor, castrato, soprano—their relationship structures the Italianate form of late seria as characteristically as the baritone/tenor/soprano triangle does Verdi's melodrama: the model of all relationships, whether of power or of intimacy. The sudden breakdown of this configuration signals that, in *Tito,* the serious genre has ended with its hero's impotence. – In *Idomeneo,* ten years earlier, Mozart had followed the traditional vocal pattern for the last time, turning its defect into the birth of a character. The King of Crete, like the Emperor of Rome, is suffering from his double isolation as the highest and the weakest. Yet his tenorial ambivalence, his splendor and pallor, need not drop out of the drama, disintegrating into the hollow luster and craven inwardness of a royal rentier. For that is what the plot is about: Idomeneo draws his dramatic life from the dichotomy of being both aggressor and victim, tyrant and slave.

The wrath of Neptune, who orders infanticide, splits the sovereign like an ax blow into a slave of the cruel gods and into a tyrant of his dearest dependents. Artemis, Agamemnon, Iphigenia in Euripides' *Iphigenia in Aulis* are the prototype for this kind of tale. But the "teleology of the ethical" (Kierkegaard), which in that play—tragically, gloriously— justified the father's crime against his child as the general's duty toward his Greek countrymen, is no longer valid for the Enlightenment. Indeed, from Diderot's *Père de famille* to Schiller's *Kabale und Liebe,* the love of the bourgeois paterfamilias who combats the cruelty of the political is elevated to the paradigm of all virtue. – Meanwhile, the fawning genre of the seria, too loyal and mendacious to let even a villain calumniate the caprice of the prince, does permit a sovereign, reduced to a slave, to quarrel with the tyranny of the gods. Rebellious, timid, desperate Idomeneo cries out about Neptune what Sesto is not permitted even to think about Tito: "Pitiless deities!" "Barbarous, unjust Gods!" Disbelief in sovereign rule has masked itself as praise of a nonsovereign ruler; so it rests with the disbelief in Olympus to unveil the truth about the gods as sovereigns (or the sovereigns as gods?): to condense pain and insight into a brooding arioso, into the choked cries of the recitative. Out of Idomeneo's wounded music, his human countenance becomes hallucinatorily alive. Does the god who wounded him also come alive?

The far-echoing, mighty lament of Monteverdi and Gluck, in which the godlike man invoked the manlike god, is denied to the latecomer *Idomeneo*. The Agamemnon prototype may endow the opera with a human world of stunned agony, but it can no longer spread above it a heaven teeming with personal gods. Neptune's wrath and mercy are the stuff of fable, not the truth of *Idomeneo*. Its shocking reality of pestilence, the rebellion of nature and the populace, of tormented hysteria, exhausted suffering, and ineffable consolation unfolds only within the enclave of operatic myths and legends, protected by the admission that these are purely fictitious. The idea of granting seria the asylum of fiction in the age of skepticism was shaped by the opera devotee and skeptic Baron Grimm in, of all places, his review of Lemierre's tragedy *Idoménée* (1764). To be sure, he starts out with the rudest scorn for God, "who must sacrifice his son because he once allowed an apple to be eaten." Heathen and Christian belief in gods is belief in fate, and belief in fate is superstition, devised and exploited by the "fraud of the priests." Nevertheless (or for that very reason), the Idomeneus story about the sacrifice of a son is especially suited to opera, full of "a dark spirit of uncertainty, vacillation, sinister meanings, fret and fear, which torments the people and helps the priests."

Eight-year-old Mozart happened to be staying in Paris when his protector Grimm defined the basis of seria thus: belief in what has ceased to be worth believing.

5

Through no less than four versions, Mozart kept cutting Neptune's oracular speech in order to retain some fictional credence for the god's tergiversation: "lest the listeners become more and more convinced of his nullity" (to Leopold, November 1780). – Mozart's humans, meanwhile, are terribly credible. Never again with such obsessive meticulousness would he shape his phrases to fit every fluctuation in words and feelings; never would he so deliver up his *personae* to the aching ambiguity of the keys, to the unstable gliding off to distant notes within each key. The drama grows out of shifting lights and shadows of mood, not from solidification into characters. Thus it shows no resistance to fate, but only sullen dejection; no courage for deeds, but only trepidation after a fright endured, which anticipates a fright to come. *Because* they are not "characters": what souls these are that approach us, as from some northern land, some later century—Idomeneo, worn out by life, crippled by his foreboding of calamity; Idamante, boyishly helpless in lonesome defiance; Elettra, wild with the bitter knowledge of having been born to misfortune, reeling between the fury of hopelessness and the euphoria of self-deception. Locked in their grief, they hide from each other their constraints and desires; no confession is allowed to ease this burdened race. – *Idomeneo,* not *Tito,* suffered the acutest crisis of the old opera. Once seria has lost its faith in the freedom of the One (in god's godliness, in the sovereign's sovereignty), it dwindles into a simulacrum of unfreedom for all.

To bring the serious genre to completion one last time

with its immense span between wrath and mercy, Mozart turned neither to gods nor to princes, but to nature: the raging storm, the gentle winds. Terror rends air and sea in the hurricane choruses. Whole again, the world breathes in the sigh of woodwinds, the whisper of strings when Idomeneo rests on the long-sought shore, when Elettra dreams of sailing toward happiness, when Ilia teaches the "zefiretti" about love. Yet while Mozart's errant masterpiece is delivering the divine stick figures of the decaying opera seria into youthful pantheism, a new kind of deliverance appears in the human sphere as well. Ilia brings a solution to the dejected tribe of *Idomeneo* that frees them both from their curse and from their genre. Boldly, the enslaved woman breaks the law of silence that weighs on all pawns of fate as she declares to her doomed friend: "I love you, I adore you, and if you want to die, my sorrow will kill me first!" A prisoner from Troy, she is a stranger to Crete, but gloriously at home in life amid so many strangers. In her readiness to die and certainty in life, she ends her jailors' imprisonment: "The gods are no tyrants, all of you are misinterpreters of the divine will!" Such a decision compels mercy from above by making it almost superfluous. Its voice sounds like those of Konstanze and Pamina: protagonists of a new drama, they take the leading role in the play of probation and autonomy rising.

The singspiel reserves all its sympathy for the average man. Because of such partisanship, *Die Entführung aus dem Serail* has no music for the noble Pasha Selim. Not with his *clemenza* prose, protesting that it is "a far greater pleasure to repay injustice with kindness than to requite vice with vice"—not through "so much grace" of the sovereign—is the happy outcome of the abduction concluded. The *peripeteia* has been wrought *earlier,* by the subordinate who ceases to be one. Through a vocal leap filled with the ecstasy of her will, driven in the repeat up to high B-flat, Konstanze in that unprecedented duet of loyalty and death decides: "Und ich soll nicht mit dir sterben? Wonne ist mir dies Gebot." She chooses to die with Belmonte: "a blissful imperative." Yet it was solely Mozart's and Stephanie's choice to follow this outcry of self-determination instantly with the answer of forgiveness; they added the *clemenza* ending onto their otherwise faithfully plagiarized source. Bretzner's operetta *Bellmont und Constanze* had ended with a family idyll, the recognition scene of Selim and Bellmont as father and son—snugly in keeping with the sentiments of bourgeois theater reform. But it was precisely with *Die Entführung,* where autonomy first became song, that Mozart made mercy, *Gnade* (etymologically, "inclining down to help"), the guiding obsession of his future dramas. At the same instant that he rejected gods and princes, he dared to preserve mercy as the earliest promise of opera, to rescue its rescuing power.

The paradox was noted at the premiere. In those "changes in Bretzner's catastrophe" by which the model of every future German singspiel fulfills its meaning, the critic Schink suspected an assault (not just aesthetic, but political) of the old opera upon the singspiel: "Instead of a picture of life, we are given here adventure novels, whose only use is to teach us to admire false greatness." The apologist for the new genre, then, thinks it less true to "life," less plausible, that a ruler might for once forgive his enemies than that a renegade from Spain should find his lost son in, of all places, his own harem. Mozart, however, disdained to turn the singspiel, as a "picture of life," against the opera of "those interminable clemencies" (as Diderot had turned the *drame bourgeois* against the *tragédie classique*)—and his refusal rid the genre of its dogmatic narrowness and philistine domesticity. He set middle-class love and courage in the dimensions of those three great actions, plot-lines, that beg for mercy, imitate mercy, and supplant mercy: *conspiracy, rescue,* and *probation.*

((

In these three acts, the history of mercy unfolds. Ever since the myth of the Fall, the mark of conspiracy has been branded upon all deeds that provoked wrath from above. Clemency from above in turn was praised as an antidote to punishing severity, notedly when religious litigants played the New Testament off against the Old, their novel beliefs against ecclesiastic or secular law. Luther's Pauline Christology sowed written or engraved antitheses of *Gesetz und Gnade* across Europe, equating his own cause with that of salvation against sin, grace against law. If absolutism wanted to protect its own law from religious civil war, it had to ban all theological weapons and sequester that antithesis. The prince was promoted to godlike disposer of both law and grace, judgment and mercy. The subordinate of the Baroque state, for his part, was sinful (and human), as the born conspirator: the toy of judgment and mercy.

Whenever opera took up the cause of humans instead of gods, of subordinates instead of princes, it infused what was condemned (and pardoned) from on high as conspiracy with the dignity and pathos of rescue. The "opera of rescue" did not owe its program to the zeal of Méhul, Lesueur, or Cherubini, who crowded the stage of the French Revolution with (un)conquerable prison towers, dungeons, robbers' caves. Rather, opera had been reconceived so as to become the opera of rescue. Its message and mission first appeared in that primordial *favola* where the liberator led his abducted one, the husband his wife, out of the underworld and home into the light.

Die Entführung, like a multicolored ribbon, ties together the seria liberation in *Orfeo* and the high seriousness of freedom in *Fidelio*. One could say that Mozart merely redecorates the weeping vaults of Hades as an azure-draped drum-and-triangle Orient; yet he is already turning Belmonte and Konstanze's conspiracy of rescue into the autonomous probation of bourgeois subjectivity. In a joyous balancing act, this singspiel creates its middle and mediating position, keeping the same distance from the submissive entreaties of the neoclassical singer/hero as from the horn-elated "in tyrannos" stretta of the modern wife as rescuer. That which applies to the hero or heroine also applies to his or her unspectacular antagonist. Pasha Selim does not compete with either divine Pluto or monstrous Pizarro; but among operatic rulers almighty he is the first, possibly the last, sensible man.

Die Zauberflöte is to unite the venture of true love and the blessing of the ruler, autonomy and mercy, in a far stranger way. It interweaves the singspiel's sympathy for the common man with the fondness for the fabulous in Viennese popular farce. This odd and enthralling genre, peopled with magicians and craftsmen, elves and clowns, retained deep into the nineteenth century a childlike, motley belief in kindness, pardon, bounty from above. Such fairytale luck seems to remove *Die Zauberflöte* from our inquiries, making a spoilsport of anyone who would interrogate about politics and constitutional law this splendidly awkward mix of daydreaming poetry and cobbled prose.

But the dogmas and rumors of the decade around 1791 (that unique rift in time through which both reason and demagogy, revolution and totalitarianism have come to us) did not happily evaporate in Mozart's magical-heroical-farcical fantasy; rather, they crowded together here as nowhere else, uninhibited and chaotically manifold. Because even the miraculous absurdities of *Die Zauberflöte* were engendered not by the timeless joy of spinning a tale but by the sudden eruption of autonomy, they bear witness to the ruptures of the new era and the disruption of the old. We will speak of fractures in form, clashes in content—and only at the end of promises and harmonies.

((((

The Empire without Subordinates

Wen solche Lehren nicht erfreun,
Verdienet nicht, ein Mensch zu sein.

Schikaneder

I

In an attempt to contain the chaos of its own multiplicity, *Die Zauberflöte* presents itself as one single, simple action: a course of probation. Yet its structure remains incomprehensible if one ignores that it begins as an opera of rescue—and ends right before intermission as an opera of conspiracy and mercy. Probation and approbation do not occur until later. And so, in the first finale, all the elements of seria pass on stage in a gaudy farewell parade: in the outer court, the rescuer/conspirator Tamino expresses pride and doubt in his mission; he sings plaintively to his lost one, calling "Pamina!" instead of "Euridice!"; twice over, Orpheus-like, he tames wild animals and the black armies of the underworld; and he hails his beloved's approaching liberation. But then the ruler Sarastro enters to a clamorous fanfare; the wrongdoer Pamina confesses on her knees; mercy appears as a princely renunciation of both love and vengeance; and it all ends with the good old laudatory chorus. – Two episodes, however, are new, and will renew it all. Both occur at the border of Utopia: when Tamino arrives, when Pamina flees. The second moment, shining with a familiar radiance, is the miracle of *anticipation:* Ilia's, Konstanze's, and now, immeasurably greater,

Pamina's decision that predicts and compels mercy from above. The tremulous question in the midst of peril, "Was werden wir nun sprechen?" (What shall we say now?) is cut short by the brightest turning point in the history of opera and of the human subject: "Die Wahrheit, die Wahrheit, sei sie auch Verbrechen." Thou shalt speak the truth, even if it were a crime—yet *her* truth, Pamina's own truth, is not repentance but self-discovery. It lends the confession and the pardon, which now conventionally ensue, a heretofore unknown dignity. This audible presence of dignity cannot be contested, however much the *Zauberflöte* ideology merits our distrust with its split world of good and evil, with the group worship of its proprietors of wisdom.

The collective that praises Sarastro sounds totalitarian: "He is our idol, to whom all are devoted." Not long before this, in the face of such propaganda Tamino had flung the words "He is a monster [*Unmensch*], a tyrant!" But the indictment no longer applies. For in that very scene in the outer court, the hero, the values, the plot of the drama have been revised completely. Before Pamina's decision in favor of her own truth, the first all-renewing moment that severs *Die Zauberflöte* from tradition is Tamino's desertion to the alien wisdom. For fourteen scenes, one-third of the score, the plot has been heading (so scholarship teaches and denies) toward an abduction: the rescue of a good fairy's daughter from her imprisonment by an evil magician. Then Mozart and Schikaneder, in the middle of their work (perhaps after the success of another singspiel that was too similar), changed everything into its opposite. By the first finale, the "starblazing queen," originally "a good, tender mother," is suddenly no more than "a proud woman" who has "ensnared" Tamino. The "mighty evil demon," for his part, the "voluptuary villain" whom

Tamino had sworn to kill, makes his entrance as the kindly king of the priests. – We are not concerned here with the debatably sudden creation of this rupture but with its unshakable, two-hundred-year survival. The "rupture" has long since become the law, not an accident of *Die Zauberflöte*. It has turned the world of that tale into the birthplace of ideal mankind, hence into the battleground of real civil war.

The feud between the Queen's realm of night and Sarastro's empire of the sun would be classed by any international law as a war between two sovereign nations. The war Tamino wages is a just war (because it began with Pamina's theft); but after he is converted by the speaker of wisdom—like everyone, to this day, who has been brainwashed by a foreign order of wisdom—he does not view his war as unjust, but as no war at all: as a conspiracy. In the semantic terms of the genre, Act I of *Die Zauberflöte* becomes retroactively an opera of conspiracy, because its finale robs it of legitimation through (Pamina's) rescue and then signals, with demagogic gestures, the approach of an ending through (Sarastro's) mercy. But how can anyone be a conspirator who is not a subordinate? The answer is analogous: Sarastro turns Pamina, Tamino, and even the Queen retroactively into subordinates and conspirators by pardoning them in the name of a supranational law. His super-nation is called *Menschheit,* mankind. Everyone, even the *Unmensch,* is a subordinate of this "better country" without subordinates. Its law is called virtue. The republic/dictatorship of the sun sees itself as mankind, since it is the empire of good. Whoever enters it must recognize the monarchy of night as the realm of evil. Evil is particular, partisan, conspiratorial; for good is, of course, universal. Even if Schikaneder and Mozart had never altered their plan, when they crossed into the empire of the sun, they allowed themselves to be brainwashed like Tamino. The "rupture" before the fifteenth scene unifies *Die Zauberflöte,* as the battle line between good and evil first unified mankind.

The unprecedented success of *Die Zauberflöte* was established within four years. In 1793, Goethe's mother wrote: "All the workmen, the gardeners, even the people of Sachsenhausen, whose children play the monkeys and lions, are going to it; we've never known a spectacle like this one." In 1794, the *Journal des Luxus und der Moden* reports that "one hears nothing but *Die Zauberflöte* wherever a violin is playing, at all the fairs, in spas, gardens, cafés, at balls and serenades," and reasons: "Something that can have this effect on an entire nation must certainly be one of the most potent fermentation agents that the goddess Fashion trickles into the quiescent cerebral matter of poor mortals from time to time to stir it up." A pamphlet of 1795, fearing cerebral fermentation, sees "(would you believe it?) that whole opera, the famous, widely known *Zauberflöte,*" as part of the "secret system of Jacobinian conspiracy in the Austrian territories." After Thermidor, even the legitimists finally understand the question of legitimacy at stake in civil wars: Who may call whom a conspirator?

2

The secret teachings about the struggle between good and evil made it known that they regarded this struggle as the civil war of the new against the old (authorized, indeed commanded, by the philosophy of history). *Die Zauberflöte* places new and old into a system of opposites with explosive propaganda potential. Sarastro is given the men's chorus with bassett horns and trombones, the Queen the trio of ladies with sparkling woodwinds. The Order is opposed to the clique, discretion to secretiveness, wisdom to *raison d'état*. The Queen rules as an absolutist monarch, not through ideology but through cabinet politics, which to Mozart's contemporaries is mere cabal, "roaming in subterranean vaults and brewing revenge against mankind." Not the attack on sovereignty but sovereignty itself is now called conspiracy. The conceptual change becomes reality: in the summer of 1791, while Mozart is writing his two operas, *La clemenza* for a coronation and *Zauberflöte* for mankind, the queen in Paris, sister of the prince to be crowned in Prague, is every day further unmasked as a conspirator against mankind. One of her ladies-in-waiting has been lynched: "To hell with the women!" The absolute state (engulfed by the progressivist stream that is flowing through all social and legal disputes, subsumed into the new, temporal vision of institutions) is sentenced to be only a momentary station, an inhuman stage in the ascent of the human race. Its kingdom of evil, which planned to "ensnare the people through fraud and superstition," must be "annihilated," must perish in "thunder, lightning, and storm."

The empire of good, however, despite our dubious experiences over the last two centuries, has been permitted to survive in *Die Zauberflöte,* full of shining persuasion. True, the workmen's and shopkeepers' dream of things to come was already confounding emancipation with repression; almost every scene mixes tolerance with the annihilation of the enemy, the idea of equality with misogyny, wisdom with ignorant rumors. And yet the figure of good is never blotted out. However soon its decodable allegory of the great struggle was superseded politically, this patchwork fairytale, weary of high art, continued to produce ambiguous meanings, riddles of plebeian intimation and sectarian hope. Yet in their critical chitchat, the middle-class up-starts, proud of their recently acquired cultural refinement, tried to free Mozart's precious gift from the talk of the rabble—to separate "the depth, the enchanting heart and soul of the music" from the "wretched" libretto. – But when the notes are separated from the text, it is the text that is liberated. Thus Pamina's formula of submission, in-herited from the seria and recast by the demagogy of the Order, "Herr, ich bin zwar Verbrecherin" (My lord, it is true I am a criminal), is not denounced by the music, nor silently passed over. Instead, from the very cry of contri-tion that the words force her to give voice to, breath and melody shape a song of new self-confidence, soaring with that ardent protest of reason and feeling by which, as Hegel claimed, "the subject proves to be the substance." Pamina's confession of guilt attests to her innocence: flight was her right, since it was her truth.

Mozart's score never rejects or neglects Schikaneder's book; nor does it (except in Monostatos's glittering noc-turnal complaint, in Papageno's sweet suicidal rancor) ever just echo it. Tenderly, firmly, now as completion, now as correction by the subject, the epoch-opening music eases the historical burden of all words (which the charmingly clumsy, unskilled German of the people's Vienna had al-ready begun to lighten). The measures following Pamina's confession teach this by profoundly fusing words and music. Pamina's humble formula, "I am a criminal," is answered by Sarastro's generosity, free of all *clemenza* formulas: "You love another very much." But not until Sarastro's bass is imitated by the solo bassoon (deep under the flutes and strings, affirming their gesture of renuncia-tion) do two half-measures encompass what cannot be said—what Tito's entire part with its private sighs and public sermons tried in vain to express. Leading out of a shadowy minor into brightness, the instruments tell of the enigma of mature melancholy: how it is at once the painful offering and the comforting reward of human kindness. Again, anticipation appears as the transient signal of autonomy: Sarastro frees himself before he frees Pamina, with the decision that the orchestra speaks for him while his voice pauses and gathers strength to repeat it: "einen andern sehr." Only after that may—must—the verdict of mercy follow: "I will not force you to love." Twice over, Sarastro's nine measures pace out *Die Zauberflöte*'s harmonic circle of teaching and reconciling (I–IV–V–I). So tangible a presence of mercy puts to shame the clattering nullity of Tito's renunciation address to Servilia, written less than four weeks later: "Ed io dovrei / Turbar fiamme si belle?" Mozart allegedly left the composition of the recitative to one of his pupils.

Criticism of Mozart's operatic forms should heed their sensuous detail, even while inquiring into the words of the libretto or the idea of the genre. The unity of idea and words (as the design for a world or the text for a coloratura) is precarious anyway. Although both idea and words precede the composition aesthetically and chronologically, their union triumphs or fails only with the birth of the music. (Thus the style-setting coherence of Calzabigi's scene "Popoli de Tessaglia" could never be proved by the existence of Mozart's concert aria alone, without the sublimely sorrowful oration of Gluck's Queen Alcestis.) To grasp our particular problem—what opera becomes when all ideas and words begin to change—we should listen even more intently to what the sounds are telling us. We need to test whether the breakthrough of mercy (which seria, singspiel, and buffa promised and spelled out, each in a different way) has been proved true, or given the lie, by its own music. – In

Tito, the praise of sovereignty made the music of mercy sound untrue. In *Die Zauberflöte,* the rise of autonomy helped mercy come true. This double paradox forces us to confront at last our most perplexing question: In the era of autonomy, what need is there for mercy?

3

The act of autonomy, around which German classicism assembled itself, is modeled on magic, not on instrumental reason. This act knows, wishes, *effects* that the individual, by the sheer decision to affirm his or her own truth, is able to change his destiny, to burst the prison of fate—otherwise freedom would be only an enticement to failure. "Anticipation" itself, the sequence of binding and releasing, of self-discovery and happy ending, is nothing but the dramatist's abridgement of that transcausally magical conjunction. When Goethe's Iphigenie, Mozart's Pamina confess, celebrate their truth "even if it were a crime," they do not cause but rather compel (through the ritual of their offer to die) pardon from above. To be sure, only the utopian mind would recognize this as the newest Covenant, which liberates what is above as well as what is below, uniting both in humanity. The empirical mind sees the response of mercy as an alien caprice, or just coincidence. Bondage to fate can, absurdly enough, be broken only by the favor of fate; the individual can round his existence into a whole only, as Goethe put it, "if quite unexpected things from outside come to his aid." Piously believing this and bitterly accepting it, Goethe entrusted self-realization in his life to the "daemon," in his major work to the devil. – *Die Zauberflöte* attempts to draw self-realization, as the whitest magic, tamed but undiminished, into the probation process of its plot and music. Magic, however, breaks forth as an arrogant, totalitarian mystagogy, splintering that process into the most fragmentary on Mozart's stage—just when the hopeful certainties of magic should be converted into the claims for just reward of probation.

Although *Die Zauberflöte* is the exemplary opera of probation, it is founded on the alliance of autonomy and mercy in Pamina's and Sarastro's dialogue of the first finale. In Act II, the truth of that first reconciliation turned to music should be reaped by the secular, immanently human nexus of probation and reward. Yet Mozart cannot compose it. His hero keeps silent, yields speech to the priests, who are determining his self-determination. The ever more disparate instances of inspired music are not evoked by the stages of Tamino's Masonic climb up the ladder of achievement, which would penetrate even to Eleusis "by effort and diligence." Instead, they accompany Pamina's unguided travels through suffering, as she strays through zones of revenge and forgiveness, rape and true love, madness and courage in the face of death—until the moment when the woman in need of rescue, herself now the rescuer, can call out "Tamino mein!" Some neo-Marxist preachers among musicologists have reproached Tamino for surviving his trials only through Pamina's "cheating" with the magic flute, thus blackening the very glory of the conclusion. For a few seconds, the elitism of male bonding is overcome by the powerless woman's undaunted dignity. She offers to humanity the talisman of her weakness, to guard it from the arrogance of the new bourgeoisie that pretends to be all of humankind. – *Humanität* of the first Classical period (Goethe's and Mozart's completeness, which was itself a call for completion) could probably be conceived of only in the brief alliance of the noble and the bourgeois that arose in Weimar and Vienna under the protective construct of enlightened absolutism.

What endures of the Classical achievement may well be an ideal image of that political illusion's very transience: not the delusion of Mozart's (Tito) seria, but the utopian expectation of his (Sarastro) singspiel.

Utopia's Constitution is spelled out in the aria "In diesen heil'gen Hallen," or more precisely in the twofold unity of the Queen's aria of revenge and the Priest's song of forgiveness. If listened to separately, Sarastro's declaration loses its edge. For here, as in both the Declaration of Independence and the Declaration of the Rights of Man, the new law resides in a counter-manifesto. Mozart's most positive creed springs from negativity. The two mottos, assertion and contradiction, are yoked with a pun: "Der Hölle Rache kocht in meinem Herzen" (*Hell*'s vengeance boils in my heart) and "In diesen heil'gen Hallen kennt man die Rache nicht" (In these holy *halls* we know no vengeance). Their literal and figurative opposition and cohesion bespeak a programmatic aim, which Mozart's theater, intent on sensually nuanced animation, otherwise shuns. Its signifiers are the two most extreme tempi of the score (Allegro assai and Larghetto), the harshest clash of tonalities (D minor and E major), the rift between the two registers that spans four octaves from low F-sharp to F above high C (about all that can decently be sung on stage). The acoustic extremes are emblems of the range of a political/dramatic design that after 150 years—bypassing *Tito*—conjures up and exorcizes the spirit of *Cinna*. Revenge reclaims its historical dimension (as "pre-history" since the Erinyes/Eumenides); and forgiveness becomes again the paradigm of founding a state. Each of Sarastro's acts of mercy, far from being routine *clemenza,* holds meaning as the memory and the renewal of the establishment of the Empire of the Sun—of the birth of humanity, which stopped the poisoning of the world by vengeance.

The founding of a real state in *Cinna* ended the civil war, for a while. We still do not know whether the founding of a utopian state in *Die Zauberflöte* initiated an endless civil war between new and old, good and evil—or eternal peace.

☾

Die Zauberflöte's later history, rife with horrors, still needs to be written. As early as 1796, Goethe, displaying a prophet's perfidy, chose the very singspiel of humanity to exemplify the new social and cultural arrogance of piano-thumping merchant's daughters, in *Hermann und Dorothea.* In 1815, Schinkel's stage offered no counterpart to such conventional and impervious self-satisfaction in higher things, but rather its purified, essential monument. For the dazzling threat of his twelve set designs radiates not from their romantic cliffs and chasms but from the surreal calm, torpor, that weighs on each ideal landscape. *Die Zauberflöte,* like no other work of art, helped the German bourgeoisie transform the "better country" into a different one: the theatrical island of the good, true, and beautiful, encircled by floods of pragmatic barbarity. Anyone who as a child listened to the "Hallen" aria sung by the Reich's basses Strienz, Hann, Weber in broadcasts from unholy national memorial halls, offering "strength through joy" to a murderously triumphant *Wehrmacht,* will never again hear that tune without anguish or shame. The whole teaching then lay in the words of simplicity monopolized by the Order: "Anyone not cheered by these teachings / Does not deserve to be a man."

The promise of *Die Zauberflöte* has been more truly kept by its precursors than by its heirs. The tone of "Wo Mensch den Menschen liebt" (Where man loves man, / No traitor can lurk, / For we forgive our enemies)—this voice of reconciliation echoes far back, even beyond the expedient *pax* oracle of Corneille's Livie—who serves the state by decreeing that henceforth neither prince nor subordinate need fear one another. It was Montaigne who knew how to retell Seneca's lesson in mercy, and end it like a comforting old bedtime story (in Florio's version): "Now after this accident, which hapned to Augustus in the xl. yeare of his age, there was neuer any Conspiracie or Enterprise attempted against him; and he receaued a iust reward for his so great Clemencie."

☾ ☾ ☾

The Society of Sounds

Là mi dirai di sì . . .

da Ponte

I

Comic operas do not end with an act of mercy. Surprisingly, of the best (from the eighteenth century up to the twentieth) only two end with an act of forgiveness: Mozart's *Le nozze di Figaro* and *Così fan tutte*.* Forgiveness is the mask worn by Mercy when, as a refined, distrustful guest from the seria world, she accepts an invitation to the marriage feast prepared by the shrewder, mocking spirits of the buffa. Her fear of derision seems all too justified. At the end of *Così fan tutte,* the two women, wailing puppet-like in parallel thirds, lodge a grotesquely heartrending plea for mercy as they kneel to the two men—who by right should be defendants, not judges, in the trial of the sexes. Even *Figaro,* for a while, is swollen with dubious wrongs and false amnesties. The Count must be blackmailed into pardoning his rival Cherubino (I, 7); the Countess's first pardon of her jealousy-ridden husband (II, 9) is based on fraud and needs to be bargained for in 160 measures of superbly endless tug-of-war music. Whether from opportunism, desire, or complicity, Figaro's

---

*Figaro's conclusion of forgiveness was imitated thievishly in Cimarosa/Bertati's *Il matrimonio segreto,* with saccharine piety in Strauss/Hofmannsthal's *Arabella.*

letter trick, Susanna's coyness, Barbarina's disobedience are forgotten, not truly forgiven. – Only at the end does Mercy, sublimely unconcerned about future injury and grief, take off her protective mask and step into the solemn torchlight of truth and marriage. But the face that now shines forth is identical with its mask (as the Countess could resemble Susanna, because Susanna had always resembled the Countess): when all hopes of the buffa come true, then mercy *is* forgiveness.

Le nozze di Figaro, as I contended at the outset, deals with a presumption of inequality in the buffa community of equals, with the heretical claim to inborn, ineradicable difference between men. The Count's hubris, just before the end, mounts to a delusion verging on madness: that he, as sovereign, has discovered a conspiracy and may pass judgment on it. Were he the ruler of the seria, he would now, at the moment of his greatest power, have to exercise *clemenza:* forgive. The last scene of the last finale grows into a wildly chaotic dispute about the word and the substance of *perdono.* It leads to the risky finding that His Grace, whose office should be to show mercy, is not just merciless, but is the only one in need of mercy. Fallen from grace, he shouts in godforsaken, inhuman blindness, against everyone's plea for pity, his sixfold "No!" – Only now do things change; following this monstrous wrath, the buffa is granted pure music of entreaty and appeasement, such as is denied to Mozart's seria fables about wrath, entreaty, and appeasement. After the Count's "Contessa perdono!", which is a profane prayer, and the Countess's answer "dico di sì," which is secular grace, mercy itself seems to glide down to earth in the unison of the violins. Their descending eighth notes are softly woven into the ensemble's song, not as a didactic illustration but like a long-lost benediction in the language before Babel.

Le nozze di Figaro does not take place in Beaumarchais' France, Mozart's Austria, or in their censor-proof putative Spain; all of the names are Italianized. Mercy answers to the name *perdono*—not the divine *grazia,* the princely *clemenza,* nor the servile *pietà*. Yet its meaning is far from merely private. *Perdono* dwells in a noninstitutional public sphere whose obligations arise only from a shared life: society. For four acts, all the secrecies of the intrigue have been striving for this open space, where everyone becomes witness and guarantor of the last "perdono" as the chorus repeats the melody of the Countess's merciful "yes." The Catholic critic Hocquard noted that the chorus here echoes a chorale—and promptly canonized its music of bliss as sacred music. In truth, however, it is the chorus that subsumes the chorale: fulfillment in society absorbs all past devotion of believers. Society, in these very measures, constitutes itself as pure immanence, a world of free men and women. Its happiness is based on the equation of nature with reason, reason with nature. This is the oldest, most fundamental equation of the middle class, which had always used nature (the artisan's intimacy with his material) and reason (the merchant's calculation of risk) to define and legitimize itself against the military, ecclesiastical, or administrative caste. Thus, Menander's New Comedy—which happily ends with youthful marriage, that victory of nature and reason—has remained the most bourgeois and unchanging genre in European literature. But not until the last *Figaro* finale was it permitted to assert and to prove that its little world is the whole world, its society mankind. This is what immanence means.

In Mozart's buffa, reconciliation prevails as a purely immanent force: no transient bridge between above and below, but rather the daily interaction of equals as a test of possible humanity in the world of human beings—the only world they have. They know of nothing external to it; no god, no sovereign, no esoteric order, no "quite unexpected things from outside" will come powerfully and wonderfully to their help. The old mechanism of comedy is re-animated by its often-forgotten meaning, as autonomy in the concrete: each person strives for his or her self-interest, and the sum total, the ensemble, attains the happy end.* – And yet Mozart's rescuing vision, at the end of *Figaro,* preserves the divinity of mercy within the humanity of forgiveness. In the giddy amazement of the scales at "O cielo! che veggio!" circling in melodic minor until their staccato spin creates the feeling of standstill—in such interruption of human time the irruption of the timeless lives on, as wonders do in the wonderment of the ensemble.

2

The ensemble, that least totalitarian of totalities, is the heart of Mozart's buffa operas. One cannot tell whether their worlds are utopias, or whether (almost uniquely in modern art, next to Chardin and Guardi) they are quite immersed in the present, exempt from utopian longing. Which is to say, their happiness does not wait for the arrival of the happy ending. It is alive in the gift of all the characters to express themselves utterly, as a shiningly complete presence in the relationship each creates with

*That such individual striving lead to general happiness is vital to comedy. Although this sequence is impeded by pedantic zeal and strict accounting in *Die Zauberflöte* (on the eve of the nineteenth century), in *Le nozze di Figaro* the advent of happiness is still gloriously immediate. Here bliss surpasses the measure of any meritorious achievement or achievable merit. Musicologists would do well to seek out and identify Mozart's techniques for producing, within the strict forms inherent to his style, the feeling of unexpected, overflowing abundance.

every other, whether friend or foe. Happiness in Mozart's buffa means ultimately only that someone's wishes and hopes are fulfilled—and never that self-exertion is rewarded, that someone, by an act of clenched will, subdues an indifferent or unfavorable outer world. First and foremost, happiness means that all dwell closely together in love and strife (and thus learn how rightly to wish and hope, not in solitary, terroristic yearning). The philistine element of *Die Zauberflöte* can be measured by this scale. It lurks not so much in Tamino's subservience to the Order and the rules as in the delusion of abstract autonomy: that a man under alien control still takes pride in being sufficient to and responsible for himself. Not collectivism but petty-bourgeois individualism makes the German biddable, obedient to an ethics that transfigures sour drudgery into the solipsistic ecstasies of duty and discipline. The happiness of buffa, however, is Mediterranean, not because of dreamy atmospherics but because in those regions, far away from Luther and Kant, the individual and society never saw themselves as opposites.

Happiness is a category of the society rather than the individual; indeed, it is the essence of sociability, which Hofmannsthal, weighing what Western art has given us, praised as the blessing of comedy. Mozart built his society (or rather, his metaphor of happiness as sociality) out of current Italian forms, the buffa ensemble and the seria alternation between aria and secco recitative. That music never should stop becomes the purpose of the secco—it keeps comedy flowing rather than drying it up. It prevents the characters from stepping out of the completeness of the musical flow into either the mere prose of outer reality or the mere lyricism of innermost solitude. The characters must ceaselessly express their inner selves, and their discourse becomes deed. Because emotion thus speaks, and speech thus acts, an undivided identity as from before the Fall pours out of the essence of dramatic music (not quite lost until Tristan, Pelléas, and the triumph of the orchestra). This is why the routine comparisons of the dramatist Mozart with Shakespeare are vague and unfeeling. Mozart's characters do not conceal an inner space for dissembling, nor are they separated from each other by zones of pale ambiguity; the outline of one forms the boundary of the other. To be sure, they can (consciously) lie to one another. But—whether Figaro, Leporello, or Guglielmo— their farcical exaggeration of every lie is a shrill warning, both to us and to themselves, not to get lost in the foreign land of deception. Only Giovanni differs; but his music, shockingly, still does not dissemble. Not a single note in his marriage vow to Zerlina, "Là ci darem la mano," or in his declaration of love to "Elvira, idolo mio," suggests that he does not believe what he is singing. And the fact that Mozart would not, could not show what it means to live a lie—this absence of the abyss (or: fulfillment is right under your nose)—is what creates the abyss in *Così fan tutte*.

The seamlessness of the characters and the closeness of their interplay are the highest blissful intent and achievement of Mozart's buffa; yet no one conflict is whitewashed for fear of ruptures. In fact, conflicts are shown, as never since, in their full reality, uncurtailed by ideology. The foe is no less alive than the friend. Thus, *Le nozze di Figaro* shows class conflict in all its rich detail, but stops short of inciting civil war. – The enemy is the Count, who, as one against all, places himself outside society, seemingly even outside the society of sounds. Deaf to the organ-timbred call for reconciliation in the middle of the play—"Deh, Signor, nol contrastate!"—he sings against that phrase which, alone among so many false appeals and pardons, already turns the message and dignity of the final pardon into music. His "contrasting" does not go unpunished. The ruler exiled into the republic of buffa must suffer comic disgrace, which (except in one instance that I will take up soon) exceeds in cruelty any tragic chastisement of the enlightened stage. "Signor *contino*": at the very outset of the play, words and music predict that the grandee will be diminished—and that the master is not intended to grow into a villain, but to shrink into a human. The vice-addicted protagonist's punishment, his being taught a lesson, and his incorporation into the community are part and parcel of the most time-honored resolution in comedy. But is it therefore just as perverse to interpret *Figaro* as a revolutionary play attacking the nobility's rule as it would be to assert, for example, that Molière's *Miser* aims at abolishing private property?

In its aggressiveness, this comedy of Mozart (and Beaumarchais) exceeds the rest of New Comedy as tamed and civilized from Menander to Molière; this it owes to its one-class form and two-class plot. Their contradiction sets *Figaro*'s own comic genre in antithetic relation to the alien serious genre. With its Count raging about in the world of his inferiors, this opera buffa thematizes and refutes the basic tenet of all late seria: that the pity of the one who is more equal than others suffices to expiate inequality. Thus the unique *Le nozze di Figaro* comes to appear, in its characters and actions, as a polemical inversion of the paradigmatic *La clemenza di Tito*. To begin with the title, the rebellious servant, not the gracious master, is the hero; reconciliation is sealed not between sovereign and subordinate but between equals, not with amnesty but with a marriage. For this purpose, the figure of menace must be degraded to one of entreaty; and divine/princely wrath will be condemned once and for all as madness and despotism. – It is *Figaro*'s happy ending, the climax of the buffa, that brings about the most radical overturn of the seria. The sovereign kneels and is pardoned by the conspirator, whose plot in any case aimed for reconciliation, not revenge. Relieved not only of his guilt but also of his power, the transgressor need not go to hell amid thunder, lightning, and storm.

3

Giovanni does go to hell—because he kept challenging heaven, until the end, with the credo of Mozart's buffa: "Le ciel, c'est les autres." For him, nothing exists but other people; he is addicted to seeing, smelling, touching them. As if the unleashed spirit of the buffa were driving him, he seeks the fullest, closest presence of "the other": women. True, his fall is preceded by the pain, struggle, and death of others; and in his clash with the Stone Guest pain, struggle, and death finally appear in that agonizing, gigantic distortion that we know not from music or drama but from nightmares. And yet of the characters' wholeness and expressive vigor, of their togetherness in the ensemble, nothing has been lost from *Figaro* to *Don Giovanni*. The "dramma giocoso" (Mozart entered it in his catalogue as "opera buffa") is as full of audible happiness as was the "commedia per musica." Indeed, *Don Giovanni* is the prime experiment in radical earthly happiness. The hero seizes it literally and as a principle, which for him is the same thing; for Giovanni principle is the literal, his happiness (as Kierkegaard said) is not the abstract woman or all women, but each woman. At the center of this comedy's structure is a startling paradox: Giovanni crushes the happiness of others not out of avarice, jealousy, misanthropy, but as the embodiment of happiness. – The hero of New Comedy always personifies a principle; he is a man obsessed, for his soul holds only this one principle, vice. The course of the comedy is supposed to cure him: punish him, teach him a lesson, incorporate him into the commu‐ nity. But the buffa community of *Don Giovanni* can neither punish Giovanni nor teach him; for his vice, earthly hap‐ piness, is its own law. So the uncorrected hero must be chastised, "finis comoediae," by heaven.

Ever since Tirso, Don Juan's unsaintly legend has been set in Seville. Three miles outside the city lies Aguas‐ Frescas, the castle of Count Almaviva. Mozart's figures are apt to return along with their configurations: Selim be‐ came Tito and Sarastro. The Count wants to become Don Giovanni but does not succeed, thanks to the weakness of his weaknesses. Giovanni, however, could remain an Almaviva, could share with him the farce of the impotent potentate, or even (since their every adventure goes awry on their *folle journée*) share that primeval comic device, dear to Aristophanes and the *commedia dell'arte:* unending futile erection. But because Giovanni cannot be tamed, he scares off the forgiving laughter of his partners and of his audience. – In comedy, all are stronger than one, and this is their luck. In tragedy, one is stronger than all, and this is his curse. When comedy has to face tragedy (in the "dramma giocoso"), the members of the buffa community ally themselves with heaven, knowing that their average, metaphorical luck is so much weaker than Giovanni's lit‐ eral and principled happiness. They win, but their hap‐ piness is swallowed up with him. In retrospect, by hell's afterglow, we can read the mark of crippling bourgeois prudery in features other than Ottavio's; Anna, whose me‐ lodies of sorrow retain Baroque grandeur, clings like the daughters in Lessing and Schiller not to her lover (Ottavio or Giovanni) but, paralyzed by horror and virtue, to her father. The renunciation of happiness around him both impedes and spurs Giovanni. To achieve closeness in a world that is becoming more and more impermeable, he strikes and stabs the men and penetrates the women. The late variant of his drama is rooted in one of those ignominious moments when society invents a new morality, once again exchanging the unfettered idea of its happiness for the coercive instrument of good. Such a moment gives rise to a desolate, defiant lust for evil.

Don Giovanni has been called the "last aristocrat," but he was already that in Molière. There, the nobility's rowdiness, libertinage, blasphemy against God and fathers were attacked even more pointedly, the seigneur's vices voiced more impudently. What Don Giovanni has over Dom Juan, by virtue of music and the sensualization of culture over a century and a half, is precisely nonrepresentative: the vitally pulsing instantaneity of his desires, and his entanglement in the world of his opponents. Out of the momentary interaction with his opposites grows the specific virtuosity of the role: prompt, effortless change from sweetness to brutality. The interchangeability of seduction and violence defines the blessed Giovanni singer—and the devilish Giovanni character. The dramatic moment thus meets the historic moment: a sudden, wrenching thirst for the Satan's brew of seduction and violence. In 1787 *Les liaisons dangereuses* is five years old, the first version of *Justine* is being written. The fiend in these diabolical tales both limps behind and runs out ahead of his epoch, still a libertine, already a dandy. His enemies lure him and hound him with moral posturing now Catholic and aristocratic, now priggishly bourgeois. – Mozart singularly aggravates this ambiguity between two ages: he creates from obsolete material what is most modern in his work. Once again he disdains the trivially secularizing zeitgeist, which replaced the punitive heaven with the pox in Laclos' novel, a lightning bolt in Goldoni's Giovanni comedy. The same man who once wrote of *Hamlet,* while trimming the oracle's speech in *Idomeneo,* "If the speech of the Ghost were not so long, it would be far more effective," now dares to give the longest and the greatest dialogue of his opera to a father's ghost.

Again Mozart achieves the improbable. The very idea of the seria, which had degenerated to postulates and fictions, becomes real again in the buffa. With the first chord of the overture, heaven and earth begin their immense dispute: menace and entreaty sound out as never before in music. *Die Entführung* and *Figaro* created a new song to recoup the gesture of mercy in a world emptied of gods and princes. Now the old sublime is directly invoked, and the dead god, ruler, father returns—but he knows no mercy. To say that *Don Giovanni* is rare among the operas of its time because of its tragic outcome is not sufficient. Rather, most significant is, that of the seven operas that Mozart wrote in the last decade of his life (from *Idomeneo* to *Die Zauberflöte*), in *Don Giovanni* alone is there neither forgiveness nor mercy.

4

The end belongs to the overture. Gluck, who virtually invented the form, wrote: "I think that the *Sinfonia* should prepare the spectators for the stage action and, as it were, represent its contents." Wagner observed that the overture to *Don Giovanni* does the former incomparably, but neglects the latter. Indeed, listeners who trust the overture to lead them through the story will be seriously misled at its turn from judgment to jubilation. Wagner's quick excuse that the overture should not narrate "the whole drama, already complete in itself," but instead be "solely an ideal prologue" defuses Mozart's audacity. For the relation of the two sections, rather than transcending time, reverses it. The Allegro, with its boundless self-assertion, shoots out of the Andante's lofty and rigid hierarchy like a seed from its brittle husk: an impatient prediction that Giovanni's will shall explode the myth, the predetermined godfearing course of the plot. Even Wagner's opposition of the two sections does not encompass their substance: "A passionately elated boldness stands in conflict with an overpoweringly awesome menace." In fact, the rite in D minor (tutti strokes against plaintive violins, a punctuated half-measure beat against syncopated quarter notes) is itself a conflict, between the overpowering and the powerless, between damnation and the call for pity. Their sculptured configuration, which pretends to eternity, impresses itself ineffaceably on our memory, against the racing temporality of the D major brio. By reversing the sequence of the plot, the overture pins the listeners to the very moment when the tempo of the music, and the age of the world, abruptly changes. They are thus drawn into the dilemma of *Don Giovanni:* to spatialize time or to temporalize space—to side with fate or with emancipation.

The form of introduction plus sonata movement (which had already been used in the *Prague Symphony* to make D major thematic development arise, as if phylogenetically, from D minor funeral pomp) is expanded here into an image of the history of opera *qua* the history of the human subject. In the antithesis of space and time, of monumentality and instantaneity, this twofold work identifies the break between Baroque and Modern as the breakthrough of the subject. The Andante, abbreviating motives apparently to the point of rigidity, is a radically new quotation of the archaic Grave formula. For the last time it conjures up a solemn vision of the widest possible span, that between heaven and earth. Across this rift surges the dialogue between *Ira* and *Supplicatione,* the source since Monteverdi of all opera seria. But the Allegro drives forward in strident triumph, out of the ossified complicity between the ruler's anger and the subordinate's humility into the immanent totality of movement—the freedom of opera buffa. – The vehemence of this drive tips the buffa into a unique tragedy. More accurately, *Don Giovanni* is the tragedy not so much of Giovanni as of the buffa. The dialectic of its happiness, which Giovanni lives and which it must kill in him, has the immaculate perfection of fate. The middle class surrenders the hard-won freedom of the buffa to coercion once again, fearing the new individual's willpower, which it misconstrues and condemns as the old willful dominion. The bourgeois has always modeled his utopian vision of liberation on the splendor of his master. Now, like an eager businessman, he pays in advance for his de facto liberation; he extinguishes the utopian splendor along with the master.

Decades before the Revolution, a self-mutilating propriety is established, which combats the master's mastery less fiercely than the libertine's freedom. Enter the Stone Guest. He takes revenge on the buffa, whose immanence drove him to the grave. Mandated by the bourgeoisie, he executes both the enemy of their autonomy and their autonomy itself. The divine judgment passed on Giovanni, the end of all buffa, can be seen as an allegory of the approaching earthly one: the way of the seigneur leads, if not back to Rosina's middle-class marriage bed, to the scaffold. And yet the return of the Commendatore brings no opening to new music of a new era, but rather the third section of the overture. Giovanni's forward drive, his flight through the whole opera, ends where it began: at the mythically immobile, prohibitive commandment from above. – Not until the finale do we see fully revealed the iron bracket that fate puts around emancipation, the seria around the buffa. To determine the compound of the serious and the comic genre within the "dramma giocoso," scholars have frequently divided up its characters, sometimes scene by scene, in order pedantically to assign them to one genre or the other. But the clarity of Mozart's drama, the deep ambivalence of his tragedy, are the creation of an inspirational conceit which protects *Don Giovanni* (as Goethe and Kierkegaard knew) from analytic solution or dissolution and makes it uniquely inscrutable. Mozart devised that double gaze which frames every detail twice. The frame of the opera seria surrounds with breathtaking strangeness all the vital plenitude of the comedy, from the opening of the overture to the descent into hell. The second frame, tightly welded within the first, is the buffa view of Leporello, who claims his right to accost us unabashed, to mix with the audience.

In the first measures of the *Introduzione,* Leporello makes us his accomplices in normalcy, in his and our will to survive. We are to see the opening of the tragedy, the chiaroscuro apparition of Anna and Giovanni against a night in flames, through his eyes. In the Commendatore finale at the other end, as Otto Klemperer's unparalleled recording has taught us, only the view from below (the servant's and the spectators' perspective) makes the mirages on the stage both immense and real. The panic and grandeur of the last dispute are realized by stereophonically drawing Leporello (stammering, trembling, using his last strength to keep mind and body together) as a mediator into the acoustic foreground. – In Klemperer's 1947 *Don Giovanni* in Budapest, he placed Leporello downstage right during the *Introduzione,* and the servant's commentary tinged even the trio of the Commendatore's death with restless rhythms and straying intervals—thus forcing the audience to see and hear this death, despite the F minor emoting, as a murder. In the second finale, the closing of the frame, a serving table was set up for Leporello downstage left; squatting under it ("We are dead!"), he disrupted and completed the picture of terror. The action begins and ends with Leporello, but in neither instance does he act. He looks on, like us, in fear and pleasure. And, like us, he survives.

☾

By virtue of its theme and its moment in history, *Don Giovanni* became the strangling embrace of seria and buffa, in which both must perish. The finale drags Giovanni, with disruptive violence, toward both the buffa and the seria hero, only to separate him forever from both of them. Again, the hubris-bred "No!" from the conclusion of *Figaro* sounds out six times. It answers not the human cry for pity, but the heavenly command to repent. To the rebel's mind, however, the two conceal the same purpose. "Péntiti!" means to him to entreat, if not "pietà" like your servant, then "perdono" like your noble cousin. Giovanni's "No!" rejects above all else the forgiveness of buffa as a hollow fiction, cosmetics on the cadaver of life. He pays for his refusal: the buffa community triumphantly drew the Count down into life; heaven triumphantly pushes Giovanni down into death.

In the face of death, Giovanni fulfills the heroic model of the seria. With Agamemnon and Idomeneo he shares the agony and privilege of a demigod, above mere humanity, who must suffer and denounce the willfulness of the gods. But he also despises and overcomes those tyrannized tyrants' avid readiness to submit and to be indemnified; he names the supreme coercion not "Pitiless deities!" but "Foolish old man!" – Nowhere else did Mozart's opera dare full emancipation. The lethal outcome here denounces seria no less than buffa, the resolutions of mercy as well as of forgiveness. Giovanni's "I have no fear!" shames the Count, who stoops to the happy ending, a credulous coward. But it also unmasks the Commendatore, who enforces the ending in horror, as the devilish tyrant rather than the godlike prince of the doctrine of sovereignty; for he prefers vengeance to mercy.

When Giovanni descends to hell, all earlier operas, whether in the genre of mercy or of forgiveness, become the art of the lie. Truth now resides only in the struggle between rebellion and repression, between liberation and mythic revenge. Bourgeois culture, for all its hypocrisy and self-righteousness, never will quite forget or conceal this; henceforth, the vital force of the world dwells with evil. – *Don Giovanni* closes, as it began, by misleading the listener. After the menacing rhythm from the overture returns once the vengeful god has uttered his first threat, the motif of entreaty with its pain-wracked syncopated quarter notes also returns in the orchestra. But the subordinate, for whom the melody seems to be intended, does not sing it; above it, against it, he sings his harshly punctuated credo of disbelief, defiance. How could *Don Giovanni* end with mercy? Giovanni does not entreat.

Readings I–XVIII

We retrace the path step by step, as if a second consciousness, armed with proofs and doubts, were testing the propositions of the first. Imagine the process as reported by a polar explorer:

If Ahlin's people had not followed our trail precisely and caught up with us with food and new supplies, we would have lost everything at the farthest point of our advance. But if we had carried this surplus equipment at the beginning, we could not possibly have advanced this far. Our jubilation, then, was great, when Carlsson, with his blond shock of hair and ready smile, threw one bundle after another from his sled.

Lars Post, *Crossing the White Desert*

WRATH AND ENTREATY. Two great texts by Monteverdi have come down to us, telling of the subject matter of his music. Both of them grew into discourses on the drama, on the expressive forces that create and animate it. Monteverdi identified three dominant emotions in the soul: wrath *(Ira)*, moderation *(Temperanza)*, and entreaty *(humiltà o Supplicatione)*. To imitate them is the quest of music. In his preface to the *Madrigali guerrieri e amorosi* of 1638 (which is a tract not just on soldiers' rage and lovers' complaints, but on the very poetics of his oeuvre) the composer prides himself on having rediscovered the expressive type of wrath, lost since the ancient Greeks. His search, he says, was spurred by the intuition that "it is only opposites [*gli contrari*] which powerfully move [*movono*] our souls." This dramatic insight turned Monteverdi into a dramatist. The opposition, conflict, dialogue that he is postulating is between wrath and entreaty—for the essence of moderation, the middle emotion, is freedom from contrast and strife. When Monteverdi goes on to assign musical characters to the three emotions, he already lists the two extremes *(concitato* for *Ira, molle* for *Supplicatione)* as following and opposing each other. The middle force *(temperato)*, as the one which mediates and pacifies all conflict in the drama, has meanwhile slipped to the third, concluding position.

In his letter to a patron two decades earlier (1616), the practical dramatist is speaking. He has already defined the act of "moving" as the craft of true opera: touching the listeners' emotions by imitating human emotions. He protests against an allegorical libretto in which the winds hold their own dialogue: "Ariadne moved us because she is a woman, and Orpheus moved us likewise, because he is a man and not a wind." As he will consider wrath at length in the *Madrigali* preface, so now he speaks about entreaty, as the end of the whole plot *(favola tutta)*. "Ariadne leads me to a justified lament; Orpheus, to a justified supplication"—but where could the quarrel of winds lead our feelings? By end *(fine)*, however, Monteverdi does not mean the conclusion of the opera (both monologues were placed pivotally in the middle), but obviously the purpose of opera, the internal goal of its teleology. In lament the moving imitation of humans is completed. – If *temperato* (pedantically, that which *has been* evened out) still has a place in this kind of teleology, it is again the third place, as a mere result. Its mediation between wrath and entreaty lacks as yet the theologico-political dignity of reconciliation. Gay and unassuming, its character is realized in the choruses and dances of the last finale.

Thus, the strife of *Ira* and *Supplicatione* alone gives music its vital task and its ability, to speak in singing, *parlar cantando* (the refutation of *cantar parlando*, vain virtuosity bereft of sense and drama). Monteverdi's doctrine of emotions can be extrapolated into a doctrine of the genre: The high eloquence of seria grows out of the dialogue between the One (god or ruler), whose essence is menace, and the many, whose essence is lamentation. – Not until later, in the "seraphic peace" (Ernst Bloch), in the "silveriness" of Gluck's Elysium will *temperato* come to its fulfillment in the mirage of a blessed realm without domination, beyond the furies' threat and the singer's lament, beyond wrath and entreaty.

II

SINGING FOR MERCY. How did *bel canto* become a problem for constitutional law? Peri and Rinuccini's *Euridice* (1600) shows us by opposing lament with law, law with mercy (or pity). The scene is an absolute monarchy: hell.

Orfeo: Lagrimate al mio *pianto,* ombre d'inferno . . .
Plutone: Dentro l'infernal porte
           non lice ad uom mortal fermar le piante.
           Ben di tua dura sorte   51
           non so qual novo affetto
           m'intenerisce il petto:
           ma troppo dura *legge,*
           legge scolpita in rigido diamante,
           contrasta a' preghi tuoi, misero amante.
Orfeo: Ahi! che pur d'ogni legge
           sciolto è colui che gli altri affrena e regge;
           ma tu del mio dolore
           scintilla di pietà non senti al core . . .
Plutone: Romper le proprie leggi è vil possanza;
           anzi reca sovente e biasmo e danno.
Orfeo: Ma de gli afflitti consolar l'affanno
           è pur di regio cor gentil usanza . . .
Plutone: Trionfi oggi la *pietà* ne' campi inferni,
           e sia la gloria e 'l vanto
           de le lagrime tue, del tuo *bel canto.**

The dispute leaves undecided whether the ruler who in
pity breaks his own rules grows stronger or weaker. Does
mercy prove or revoke the omnipotence of the sovereign?

*Orpheus: Weep at my *lament,* shades of Hell . . .
Pluto: Within the gates of Hell no mortal is allowed to take his stance.
And yet, hearing of your hard fate I do not know what new emotion
softens my breast: but most rigid *laws,* laws wrought in hardest dia-
mond, *oppose* your pleas, wretched lover.
Orpheus: Ahi! and still, of all laws, that man is free that restrains and
rules the others; but do you at my grief not feel a spark of pity? . . .
Pluto: To break one's own laws is a misuse of power; censure and injury
are often caused thus.
Orpheus: But to ease the anguish of the sorrowful is still the noble cus-
tom of the royal heart . . .
Pluto: Let *pity* triumph today in the infernal fields, and be the pride and
glory of your tears, of your *beautiful song.*

III

TYRANT AND SOVEREIGN. Fénelon, the teacher of
princes and author of the last valid Mirror for Princes
(*Les aventures de Télémaque,* 1699), admitted to himself and
the world that "Sovereign authority is a great temptation;
every man has in him the principle of tyranny." Still, we
must be struck by how tame and tactful Fénelon's, and
even Corneille's, formulas sound, if we hold them against
the German Baroque *Trauerspiel.* Here, the ruler's godlike
wrath becomes hysterically inflated into a rage drunken
with sheer domination. "Pomposity" (which Fénelon censured even in the *Cinna* Augustus) conquers the stage in a
luridly ostentatious pageant of costume and language, led
by a clownishly staggering and bellowing gigantic bogey-
man who craves omnipotence.

Impressed by French courtesy and courtiers' servility,
Europe chose to cover up what it had learned about
princely omnipotence—until of the ruler's controlling
powers only self-control was left. After 1750, the *clemenza*
of Metastasio's title was translated into German by the
insipidly private *Mildigkeit* or *Gütigkeit* ("gentleness" or
"kindness"). – To be sure, the tyrant of the older drama,
whom the new court poets hoped to exorcize through flattery, had known nothing about *clemenza:* "Whoever of-
fends us shall be hanged, burned, put to the wheel, shall
drip blood and be drowned in the Styx *(he throws everything over in a heap and exits angrily).*"

IV

THE KIND RULER. Until around 1700, the phrase "le
bon Dieu" was used (according to Ariès) only in nursery
talk of parents to their children. It prettified the true state

of affairs, which the little ones would soon enough come
to understand.

IUSTITIA VERSUS CLEMENTIAM. During the Renaissance and the Baroque, West European city halls decorated
their great chambers with painted exempla of justice. Difficult judgments (Solomon), the punishment of unjust
judges (Cambyses), the discovery of hidden crimes, the
unmasking of false witnesses: these paintings, often arranged cyclically, exhorted the courts of law to all sorts of
scrupulous and imaginative justice, but not to clemency.
That may be because the magistrates in the city hall saw
their task as dispensing equity; the granting of "mildnesse
and lenitie" they left to the prince in his palace. – We cannot tell whether Holbein's *Christ and the Woman Taken in
Adultery* (which he painted in 1521 along with a dozen
other legal subjects for the city hall in Basel) was an exception: whether it was to inspire the magistrates with supra-
judicial mercy, or merely with judicial caution. In any
case, this parable did not recur until 1720, in the city hall
of Maastricht. "As far as we know, this is the first time
since Holbein's day that a work commissioned for a Hall
of Judgment exhorts moral [!] clemency" (K. Simon,
Abendländische Gerechtigkeitsbilder, 1948).

After that date the *exempla clementiae* in town halls mul-
tiply. The favorite subject is the continence of Scipio. This
subject, however, does not originate in the city; it is im-
ported from the princely residences. There, clemency has
begun to supplant all other topics. When in 1764 Cochin
seeks royal virtues for four supraportes in Choisy, he finds
Justice, but then the fashionable alternative three times:
Mercy, Mildness, Clemency. In 1788 Wink paints three

Scipio memorials for the Elector of Bavaria; all of them show the general's *clemenza,* none of them his conquests. – To understand the decline of absolutism, we must remember how it depoliticized itself and those it ruled. The memory was wiped out of those crises of rule and obedience which first gave absolutism its mandate: to end civil war. In the arts, analogously, the iconography of political necessity was supplanted by the glorification of luxurious princely activities, the most prodigal of which was clemency. The regime then looked on in surprise when the people came to see all the prince's offices as mere luxury and began a new civil war to halt the waste.

Throughout Europe, the commissions for painted justice ceased around 1790, as did those for representations of clemency. Once again there were victories to glorify: in the civil war and in the campaigns of the revolutionary, soon Napoleonic, armies.

VI

IMPOTENCE IN PUNISHMENT. Montesquieu's passionately ambiguous position (nostalgic for the pre-absolutist order, prophetic of the post-absolutist) can give us a sense of that narrow interim when absolutism ruled on the razor's edge. Even before final decades, rulers were accepted only because of what they did to weaken their rule. – Disbelievers and partisans of sovereignty both measured the sovereign's acts by the criterion of mercy, which showed to what extent he was prepared to integrate, rather than eradicate, legal and social interests contrary to his own. In the guise of his royal pleasure, he was to exert tolerance and thus buy tolerance from his hidden opponents, soon to be public. – When absolutist ideology, before 1700, praised the ruler's barter with his subordinates not as a politically useful compromise but as a miraculously arbitrary decree, it enriched Baroque images of mercy with artistic pomp and intellectual flavor. Practically though, such fiction ended by confusing the prince himself and provoking ever new theorems of law harshly critical of his despotism.

Montesquieu argues that the sovereign ought not to sit in judgment—that justice should be an independent "third power." His analysis, honed by vigilant obstructionism in the nobles' parliaments, offers four acute arguments against the monarch as judge. First, it means the end of security for citizens if the one who has the prerogative to punish also determines when punishment is to be applied. Second, it is incumbent on the monarch with the state apparatus to detect crimes—but not to decide whether or not they should be put on trial, lest he become both prosecutor and judge. Third, since confiscation of property is one possible penalty, the monarch as judge would have an unacceptable interest in conviction. – But it is the fourth and final argument that concerns us: "Moreover, he would lose *the fairest attribute of his sovereignty, that is, to dispense mercy.* It would be nonsensical for him to keep pronouncing and revoking his sentences; he would be loath to contradict himself" (*De l'esprit des loix,* 6, V).

In the end stage of absolutism, enlightened opinion (not without Montesquieu's complicity) transfigures this "nonsense" into the model of government. If *clemenza* is understood not as an exceptional right but as the everyday duty of the state, then the office of the ruler consists in canceling all sentences. Whether he or some second or third power has pronounced them does not affect the absurdity. This is attested by Metastasio, Montesquieu's contemporary. The plot of his *Tito* in fact assumes a division of power; not the emperor but the senate passes judgment on Sesto. The only difference it makes is that Titus's routinized amnesty now nullifies not merely his own authority but also that of the senate. – Montesquieu saw the problem, yet he veiled it over with that conservatism which made him the best utopian. He paired his acute distrust of the sovereign with an idyllic trust in the sovereign's old and new enemies.

His chapter *De la clémence du prince* (6, XXI) is a sentimental invocation of the ancient feudal values—glory, fealty, honor—as if we were still in the time of *Le Cid*. The high and mighty are so vulnerable to disfavor, to real or imagined loss of reputation, that they should be handled with mercy rather than severity. (That a peasant or a merchant could also use some mercy now and then Montesquieu fails to mention.) "Monarchs can profit so amply by clemency, it engenders so much love, it brings them so much glory that they should rejoice each time they find an opportunity to practice it." The chief question remains: "When is it right to punish? When to pardon?" Again, the answer comes not from the jurist, but rather from the writer of idylls (he does not consider the crisis, hoping that it will not occur): "This can be better felt than prescribed. Whenever clemency becomes dangerous, its dangers are patent; they can easily be distinguished from the weakness in the prince that accounts for his proneness to err, or his very impotence in punishment."

Metastasio's most successful libretto appeared a few years before Montesquieu's most influential book. Nevertheless, the former is a glorification of that same infirmity of the state which the latter feels it unnecessary even to warn against. *La clemenza di Tito* has no other content than "l'impuissance même de punir": impotence in punishment.

VII

SENECA TO NERO. "Your ancestor Augustus pardoned the men he vanquished in civil war. Over whom would he have ruled, had he not pardoned?" *(De clementia)*

VIII

CINNA. Profound and perplexing is the way Corneille
assembles and aggravates all the contradictions of the story
he found in Seneca, Dio Cassius, and Montaigne, in order
to construct the rupture of all ruptures: the moment when
the state is born out of a civil war. In the first act he shows
the world strictly from the viewpoint of the nobility's
noble resistance. Undaunted by king and cardinal, he disdains to resolve the great debate about whether the republic (of the nobles) or the monarchy (of their conqueror)
is preferable: the old or the new. Indeed, the proponent of
absolutism, Cinna, dissembles in his speech and actions,
thereby discrediting his own tenets. It is recorded how un-
suspectingly the first spectators from the upper aristocracy
rushed to take sides with the conspirators: Guez de Balzac
saw in Emilie a "holy and venerable fury," who "in avenging herself, avenges the entire universe." Prince Conti
rounded off this view by mocking Auguste's clemency,
which "audiences will forget even before they leave the
theater."

But however much the logic, morality, and sentiment of
individual scenes continue to defend what is passing away,
the drama unfolds wholly in the realm of what is to come;
and how the need for the ascending order turns past injustice into new justice is Corneille's topic. The artistic and
political acumen of his work, as we still can sense, is won
through the bitterest inner combat of self-denying recognition. *Cinna* is the first significant French tragedy that
ends well. Commentators concur that its tragic essence is
hard to find. It hides where no one seeks it: in the happy
ending. It evolves from the author's own tragedy of having
to admit that surrender to the merciful one means only the
(grimmest) happiness for the many. At the very end, when
mercy prevails, Corneille himself seems to congratulate

the tyrant, who henceforth must be called sovereign, with ragingly defiant humility: "Après cette action vous n'avez rien à craindre: / On portera le joug désormais sans se plaindre." Now they will bear their yoke without complaining.

Out of the wound left by the uprooting of the ancient truth was born the restorative reality of Corneille's play. At the premiere, the Grand Condé wept during the happy ending—hardly from gratitude for the monarch's pardon but rather from his own incapacity to think of any better end. His pardon eighteen years later by Mazarin was *his* end: the disarming of the noble hero, the outmoded rebel.

IX

PORTRAIT OF A SOVEREIGN (1734). In the dedication of *La clemenza di Tito* the court poet addresses his emperor, Charles VI: "Do not believe, my Lord, that I intended to portray you in Titus. True, I am told that everybody will recognize you in him. Oh, invincible Augustus, forbid, if you do not wish to see your features mirrored, forbid the Muses to commemorate heroes." Flattery becomes complete only with the painstaking demonstration that it is not flattery. "The Imperial Poet!" Alfieri soon scoffed. "The coupling of those two words begets a monster."

PORTRAIT OF A SOVEREIGN (1781). How can one make a royal portrait at least into "a painting as attractive as that of a virtuous private citizen"? Under Joseph II, the answer was "Kings interest us, of course, not as kings, but only insofar *as they are men*." And yet, "The monarch who, despite the veil of incense that flattery draws about his throne, despite the many opportunities which can so easily make him forget his humanity, still remains *always a man* and surpasses others *only as a man,* indeed, *such a man* is the most attractive painting a poet can devise" (Schink, *Dramaturgische Fragmente*).

X

SINGERS AND STATUES. The seven voices in *Idomeneo* (1781) are three tenors, one castrato mezzo, two sopranos, and only one bass, the voice from the underworld, who sings for scarcely two minutes. Then in *Don Giovanni* (1787), we have four basses, one tenor, three sopranos, and no castrato at all (though Ottavio carries some burden of that heritage). Within the briefest time, Mozart experienced a complete reversal in his vision of dramatic plots—in the very sounds he heard from that hidden stage which (as we know from his letters) always stood ready in his mind, lights on, curtain raised for new characters to enter, new words to be sung. – I have asserted that in *Idomeneo* Mozart fulfilled the seria configuration of voices for a last time; and yet it must be admitted that he saw things otherwise. He seems to have cursed the convention as much as he made use of it. *Idomeneo* was the turning point in his life and work. He was planning to escape to Vienna; in his mind he had stored up all the materials of tradition along with an explosive charge of compositional freedom. Thus at his Munich rehearsals even the most incidental of musicians' intrigues (such as plagued every opera premiere) grew to have paradigmatic meaning. Because in seria the tenor occupied the ruling position (the position of the ruler), Anton Raaff, the first Idomeneo, was at the center of these paradigms.

They called him the greatest singer of his time, which unfortunately was not that of *Idomeneo*. As late as 1792, Reichardt assured the retired seventy-eight-year-old that he had been "considered the foremost tenor in the whole European singing world and is still considered so." But fif-

teen years earlier (1777), Mozart had written from Mann-
heim about "the old tenor, *formerly so famous*": "If I didn't
know that this is the great Raaff, I would double over
laughing." The next year he wrote from Paris: "I'll admit
that when he was younger and in his prime he might have
made an impression—I like his effect, but it's too much for
me, it often strikes me as ludicrous." Three years later
(1781), the superannuated ruler of the boards, leading art-
ist of the Elector Karl Theodor's troupe, sang Idomeneo,
King of Crete. We do not know if there were disputes
about this decision; Mozart's correspondence with the
Munich court has been lost. Father and son must have dis-
cussed between themselves at least the bold idea of casting
a bass: "If I had written [the aria] for Zonca . . ." Mozart's
first reaction at the rehearsals is not to the singer, but to the
actor: "Raaff is a *statue*."

During the rehearsals Raaff was able to keep Mozart
from composing an intended ensemble; and he was unwill-
ing to sing the miraculous quartet. Raaff's refusal and
Mozart's abysmally shrewd retort—that ensembles ought
to be spoken more than sung anyway—attest to more than
the eternal obtuse cunning of star tenors, who loathe to
mingle their voices with those of the less well paid. Rather,
around 1780, the seria tenor was forced by dramatic stereo-
types and training into the same defensive posture as the
sovereigns he portrayed. Raaff, the aged virtuoso, could
no more master the requirements of collective rhythm and
intonation in Mozart's ensembles than a true *clemenza* ruler
could overcome his dilemma of being either a prince or a
man. But had not Raaff's paralysis, for once, become part
of his role? Is not Idomeneo the nonsovereign at the endless moment of his powerlessness—wanting to save, but
having to kill his son—an unhappy man because he is a
prince, and an inadequate prince because he is a man?

"Raaff is a statue": a judgment of most delicate ambiguity. The heroes of seria *were* statues; in attitudes of elevated, representative passions and sorrows they lifted their gazes, arms, voices to the gods, who like fixed stars remained unmoved. Even their virtuoso switching from one *affetto* to the other had nothing to do with a flexible psychology, with a dialectically variable interplay between person and situation. Not until a new spirit of play had arisen in the situated ensemble number (and in the ensemble of singers required by Mozart's ensembles) does the word "statue" become an insult. In Metastasio's libretti there had been only secco recitatives and exit arias, no ensembles. Mozart serves up arias for Raaff as best he can, for from Paris he remembers that "as far as bravura, passagework, and runs go, Raaff is a master"—and still before the premiere he has to simplify the music. "Concerning trios and quartets," he tells Raaff angrily, "you have to give the composer free rein"—and yet he drops an ensemble he had already sketched out.

At the core of *Idomeneo,* after all the battles lost and won over libretto and music, lies a defeat. The "wondrous work" (Brahms) has heroic scope—not its hero's, but its composer's. Never did Mozart dare more, though he often succeeded better. Indeed, in his oeuvre, which may seem to consist of perfect successes fulfilling all too tractable ambitions, *Idomeneo* represents a stirring refusal to adapt to what is feasible, to idolize the flawless product: it is an attempt without sequels, of torso-like sublimity. – Mozart must have suffered because of it. Even in the year of the premiere, the hope for a production in Vienna filled him with dreams of uncompromising revisions: "I would have *completely changed* the part of Idomenè, and written it *in the bass* for Fischer." As he had long wanted to carve his new genre out of the old one, so for a moment he tried to get a new work out of the old. The plan failed. When, years later, instead of turning the tenor king into a bass, he turned the castrato prince into a second tenor, it was merely to adapt to the opportunities of a single concert performance. Johann Ignaz Fischer, however, whose "specialty is comic and doting fathers and caricatures" *(Theater Allmanach 1782),* in the year following that failed performance, sang not the second Idomenè, but the first Osmin of *Entführung.* That too is a paradigm.

The familiar phrase makes a new, triumphant kind of sense, when, on July 30, 1782, Count Zinzendorf compares in his diary the singers of Osmin and Belmonte: "Fischer joue bien, Adamberger est *une statue.*" As the first truly non-statuary role of the musical theater, Osmin prevails: the bass has vanquished the tenor, the buffo the hero. – Mozart was able to fulfill the quest of his opera, to set the human being into time (endowing him simultaneously with subjectivity and sociability), only when he hired the bass and the bass-baritone out of the buffa troupe. There the tenor did not command center stage, and there were no castrati, not even as harem guards. The Count (not just Figaro), Giovanni (not just Leporello) grew out of that school of vitally comical, unerringly musical non-heroes, non-virtuosos. They start off and lead the great ensemble finale, the exchange and interaction of non-interchangeable characters, which da Ponte, who helped create it, saw as the heart of Mozart's buffa.

Where Pygmalion succeeded only once, Mozart succeeds time after time: in his operatic work after *Idomeneo* (leaving *Tito* aside) there is not a single figure who is not animated by a human soul, thanks to Mozart's love for his or her unique being. One exception proves the rule, when, for the last time, the old genre with lofty terror irrupts into the world of the new. Wreaking retaliation on the buffa for having sent seria to its grave, enters the revenger—the Stone Guest: *a statue.*

(Note on *La clemenza di Tito*.) That Mozart's uncertainty as to the seria configuration of voices kept growing up until *Tito* is shown by an academic dispute that has unnecessarily continued to the present day. The issue is significant: which voice was cast in which role at the premiere (that is, in the composer's mind)? In 1859 Otto Jahn claimed, on the evidence of a program sheet which nobody else has seen, that *Tito* had no castrato role—that both Sesto and Annio were sung by women: "Thereby humanity and morale gained much, the drama nothing." Opinions soon began to waver.

It was discovered that a "Signora" who sang at the first night according to Jahn's list was in truth a "Signore." So Abert changed Jahn's indication of gender, but without questioning Jahn's role assignments. He maintained by his own half-logic that the confidant's part of Annio had been sung by Bedini, the guest castrato of Guardasoni's Prague troupe, but the role of Sesto, the main antagonist of the tenor Tito, was taken by the soprano Perini. Only in 1958 did Westrup do the obvious thing: he proved the opposite from a long-known letter by Mozart, which describes the last performance in Prague. "The little duet *ex A*," Annio and Servilia's duet no. 7 in A major, "sung by the *two girls,* was encored." Annio was a soprano, hence Sesto was the castrato.

But the error lives on happily. Even in the *Neue Mozart-Ausgabe,* that colossal philological work, F. Giegling bases the score on Abert's incorrectly corrected cast list with Bedini as Annio, while in the volume of illustrations O. E. Deutsch captions the portrait of Perini as "in the role of Annio." Recent apologists for *Tito* are divided, too. Individually, they extol the masterwork; collectively, as it were, they admit by their difference that its very core was a matter of indifference to Mozart—that for him, by 1791, the triangle of tenor-castrato-soprano had lost its force and immutability.

The one-hundred-year-long error of most venerable scholars—their eye for Jahn's list and blindness to Mozart's letter—would be unthinkable indeed, if Mozart's music for *La clemenza di Tito* were decisive in its detail and convincing as a whole. It is precisely the genre's consistency, its affirmation of a world perfect unto itself, that should be transmitted by its configuration of voices. The tenor-castrato-soprano relationship established for the seria an acoustic model resplendent with virtuosity and pomp, but poor in weight and reality. It also ordered all affairs around that peculiar Baroque bond between the ruler's public power and amatory grief, which was taken for the most stageworthy of topics, the axis of the world.

With due caution, let us consider two modern analogies. By setting the part of Wozzeck for a baritone instead of a tenor, Berg refuted the Italianizing view of life and love. He freed compassion from the confidence tricks of wishful identification. Only one year later, Stravinsky's *Oedipus Rex,* by rediscovering the high tenor with his archaically flat brilliance emptied of subjectivity, announced both the end of expressionistic sympathy for the human creature and the beginning of a cruelly impassive neoclassicism, which sided not with those who suffer, but with fate.

From Osmin through Almaviva to Fiordiligi, Mozart kept renewing the character of voices and thus of genres. When he wrote his last seria, though, he was no longer able to invent (nor was the genre able to supply him with) a coherent "serious" world. He could not believe any more in tenors as omnipotent/impotent rulers, nor in castrati as hotheaded successors to or rebels against the throne, nor in sopranos as beautiful damsels universally persecuted yet ardently adored.

XI

TREATING THE INCURABLE. Any shrewd theater manager of the day could have given Mozart three prescrip-
tions for turning *Idomeneo* into a fine, successful seria—for
which there was still a market. First, the role of Neptune
must be invented, and heightened for scenic and musical
effect. Second, to save Idamante, Idomeneo (instead of ir-
resolutely betraying the god and his own vows) should un-
dertake some heroic deed that would govern and unify the
plot. Third, Ilia's act of rescue must be more than a momentary episode: it should shine out as the climax of her
steady ascent to self-sacrificing valor in the face of death.

And yet because the real decrepitude of *Idomeneo* had its
origin not in lack of dramatic skill but in the decline of the
genre, Mozart did not even try to doctor the libretto—instead, he used precisely its weakest places to test the breakthrough to unprecedented meaning and sensibility. He
transformed divinity into the newly expressive power of
destroying and healing Nature. He turned Idomeneo's pas-
sivity and half-heartedness into the beginnings of psychology in opera; and he gave Ilia the music not of a lofty
heroine, but of a woman proving her worth by spontaneity—the sister of Pamina instead of Alcestis.

These three innovative strokes give *Idomeneo* an unpre-
dictable, lifelike ambivalence. Without it, Mozart's first
dramatic masterpiece would merely exhibit the death throes
of Baroque opera—displaying an opera seria that had lost
simultaneously its three souls: the belief in gods, the freedom of the sovereign, and the subordinate's great lament.

XII

THE PRINCELIKE GOD. All decrees of dogma since
A.D. 320 should have begun with the formula, "We, God

by the grace of the Emperor . . ." When this leaked out after nearly 1,500 years, the first to abdicate was the vassal on high, then his lord on earth. Since 1806 there has been no Holy Roman Emperor.

XIII

To György Ligeti

ATMOSPHERES. No one until Debussy was able to compose the music of the air like Mozart: the blessing of the breeze, for instance, gently circling after the storm has passed. "Aura soave spira di dolce calma"—the wonder of Idomeneo's rescue is verified more reliably through music than any miracle has been by the Church. Earlier, in the tempest chorus, the elements' frenzy wrings out a barbarous cry of pain: mankind plunges back into lawlessness, into the chaos of its beginnings. – It is not only that nature in *Idomeneo* is given expressive gestures of fury and tenderness, as if it were a subject in its own right; its expressive modes also reach deep into the human soul, whose distress or bliss can be told only as the music of tempest or of calm. Thus, in Ilia's liberating confession to Idamante, her recitative is accompanied not by the orchestral hues of passionate love but by those of a *zefiretto;* thus Idomeneo's most fervent prayer to Neptune, the god of sea and storm, is not a lofty lament, a Baroque entreaty, but a utopian likeness of calmed and calming breezes, curing the world: "Wind, retire to the sea, may your wrath have an end." How far this nature music is from the disputes of allegorical winds which Monteverdi once shrank from composing.

And yet there was a strong tradition of nature depiction in the Baroque: in 1780, Schink mocks the many wrecked vessels with which German stages continued to be strewn, due to Metastasio's once fecund fancy for marine tempests.

The music of the air in *Idomeneo* is striking and strange precisely because it is still on the way to outgrowing the old manner: it allows us to measure the contrasting illustrative types of the Baroque against the novel unity of form that is pledged by the composer as subject. In both the orchestra and the voices we hear the stylistic rupture from which the youthful subjectivity of nature *and* man is about to break forth in storm and stress. – This double animation of the world is served by Mozart's discovery of the woodwinds. As instruments of wind and of breath, they voice the blissful awakening of both nature and man. From now on, beyond heightening the emotions of stage antagonists (as it continues to do right into the *accompagnati* of *Don Giovanni,* indeed of *Così fan tutte*), the orchestra provides the common air, the atmosphere that enfolds them. After *Idomeneo* and thanks to it, the ensemble as the unified, unifying medium of the three great Italian buffe can replace the artfully sculpted and contraposed tirades of seria heroes.

Thus *Idomeneo* secured for the future the reality, the startlingly new presence, of Mozart's characters. They cannot lose one another, since they are embraced by one animated world. Their connections also can no longer be reduced to the lofty relationships of seria, which stem from representative tensions between superhuman persons and/or personal gods: a dialogue between the essential positions of existence and sufferance. Now each moment brings a change in the characters' position within themselves and toward each other; along with atmosphere, time is created on the opera stage.

More could be said, about the night in the second finale of *Figaro,* singing out of the people who are enveloped by it; or about the sextet in *Don Giovanni* with its buffoonish and tragic blind stumbling about in the dark, and then, when Anna and Ottavio enter, with its torchlit proud and sorrowful radiance. And yet more about the new sensibility in *Così fan tutte*'s *terzettino,* where the murmur of the sea is blended, confounded with the soul's interior flow of time, as in poems, forty years later, of Brentano and Eichendorff. Since *Idomeneo,* nature is no longer depicted: it comes to life on stage and is lived by the audience.

XIV

THE RUPTURE. Corneille's determination to capture political reality led him to invent a dramatic device: the inversion of sympathies after the first act—no less abrupt and notorious than the one contrived during the first *Zauberflöte* finale. In both cases, our compassion for the conspirators is first carefully fostered, then betrayed. Voltaire wrote: "It is important to realize that in this first act Cinna and Emilie seize our total interest. We tremble that they will be found out. You shall see how *this interest is later changed,* and you may judge whether that is, or is not, a flaw." *Intérêt* conveys here not only "interest," but rather—as later in the theory of the *drame bourgeois*—compassion, empathy, even identification. Voltaire makes it instantly clear that he means a change of identification, of the spectator's political partisanship. Cinna is summoned by the emperor at the very moment (the end of Act II) "when he has instilled into us the utmost horror of Auguste's cruelty, when we have no other wish but that the tyrant be killed—when *every spectator feels himself to be one of the conspirators.*" Enter the sovereign; and he immediately has right as well as might on his side. We may even, betraying the traitors, award him our compassion.

The analogy to the rupture in *Die Zauberflöte* could hardly be more complete, so the difference is even more striking. We see on the one hand the breathtaking political objectivity which Corneille wrests from the duplication and change of partisanship—and on the other hand the departure from all political objectivity effected by the splendid relief of Mozart and Schikaneder's partisanship for supersovereign mankind. The rupture in *Die Zauberflöte* is the crack through which the composer and librettist escape from conflict into utopia.

XV

For Reinhart Koselleck

THE ENEMY IS ANNULLED. All politics begins by accepting the reality of one's opponent, by recognizing the justification for his position. *Die Zauberflöte* is a miscellany of enlightened nonsense about politics and sense for the unpolitical, which finds its true summation at the works' end: "The sun's rays drive off the night, / Destroy the hypocrites' fraudulent might." The opponent's belief is not even acknowledged as blind or wrong belief; it is denounced as hypocrisy—no belief at all. Its substance consists in hiding its void of substance. Accordingly, the enemy is branded with the emblem of the night: nothingness, vacuity, the mere absence of light. The French Revolution interpreted its own action, even before it began, as the banishing of the night. Since its enemies did not exist, as it were, they would fall automatically, without bloodshed. The revolution annihilates Nothing: therefore it counts nothing as a loss, everything as a gain.

In Adolph Knigge's secret-society novel, *Geschichte Ludwigs von Seelberg* (1787), there is talk of a brotherly Order of Light that has "in hand the surest means of guiding everything toward the great objective of restituting truth and freedom on earth *without violence or danger.*" The members of the order "did much *in quiet,* bringing about revolutions which were attributed to other causes." In 1789, six months after the storming of the Bastille, the metaphor of conquering darkness takes on a somewhat less peaceable tone in Christoph Wieland's novel *Peregrinus Proteus:* "The light has broken forth from amidst the darkness, the kingdom of demons and their servants is nearing its terrible end. The City of God has already come down to us . . . , the people of the earth will be gathered to it, and each of its rays will be a lightning bolt which will consume the enemies of the light." History as a show of nature is now in progress; at its climax in 1791, the Queen of the Night and her attendants will perish in "thunder, lightning, storm." Their wail, in that now self-denunciatory rhyme *Macht/Nacht,* equates domination with annihilation: "Smashed, destroyed is our might, / We are plunged in eternal night."

The metaphor of light and darkness answers the favorite riddle of today's enlightened critics who choose to ignore what the Enlightenment was. How does it happen, they ask, that Sarastro preaches pardon but, as his first action on stage, orders that Monostatos's feet be lashed "seventy-seven times"? If the critics had seen something more in this incident than their chance to display verbal brotherhood with slaves and blacks, they might have added a deeper puzzle: Why is *the* programmatic deed of *Die Zauberflöte,* the pardoning of the Queen in the *Hallen* manifesto, followed nonetheless by her descent to hell? Such lack of logic leads to the heart of the Enlightenment's revolutionary logic. The enemy, black as night, is unreal; therefore he can be whipped, damned, annulled. Humanity is valid only for humans, not for monstrous non-humans—valid, that is, only within one's own party. "Anyone not cheered by these teachings / Does not deserve to be a man." The *terreur* soon showed that splintering off from the Party (that heir to the Order of Light) meant expulsion into nothingness. Death on the guillotine was not the consequence but the verification of an annulment that virtually had already been carried out, by the apostate victims themselves.

Note. To grasp how thought suddenly changes before a civil war, we may have to refer to the physiology of aggression. Shortly before battle, the brain seems flooded with a hormone which suppresses the recognition of external beings and things in a rush of self-exaltation. This shift in mental chemistry, whether in fighting fish or humans, makes the enemy fade into his mere image—shrivels his reality into a function of the hatred and rage necessary for the attack.

XVI

PAMINA'S THREE DEATHS (1, 2). How the music and the libretto of *Die Zauberflöte* strengthen, interpret, correct each other may be guessed by the experience of a child, whose excited fantasy both rejected and outdid Schikaneder's invention. When the twelve-year-old boy first heard the singspiel, he at once fell in love with Papageno's and Pamina's exchange: "Was werden wir jetzt sprechen?" "Die Wahrheit, die Wahrheit, und sei sie auch Verbrechen." Telling the truth, here ("even if it were a crime"), was no miserable "You must" imposed by the blackmail of parents or teachers. It sounded rather like a liberating "You may": not obliging you to betray yourself, but helping you to be true to yourself. – However, the child distorted the words. He could have sworn that the wonderful maiden standing there in the light had sung out, despite the rhyme, "Die Wahrheit, die Wahrheit, und sei sie auch *der Tod*."

"The truth, even if it were death": this one moment remained the child's, the adolescent's favorite, long after he had recognized his error. – Many years later, it suddenly occurred to him that perhaps not he but Schikaneder had made the wrong choice between "crime" and "death." Might Mozart's music have intimated the false but truer word to his spellbound young disciple?

In Mozart, the dignity of probation is bordered by death. Facing Sarastro, passing the ultimate trials, Pamina proves her readiness to die—not her scorn for death. How should one of Mozart's creations scorn death, when (in a letter to his father) he called death "the key to our true happiness"? Yet Mozart is not writing nor is Pamina singing of happiness in the beyond. They experience and affirm the presence of death in the here and now, as the final obstacle and the ultimate release in their extreme probation. The music of Ilia, Konstanze, Pamina (like Mozart's letter) speaks of death as "man's true, best friend." Their own truth, which they find at the brink of death, gives to their soprano line its unmistakable fragility and strength. – The deaths that Pamina must pass through in order to attain the truth of her life are not to be abstracted into instructional grades or the pre-established stations of the cross. They are experiences. The impulse of Pamina's first experience is the unquestioned innate conviction of her right to live and love, which defies death—or rather whatever is deadly, hostile to life in an all-too-righteous world.

"The truth, *even if it were* a crime!" Crime here does not mean evil deeds, harmful to gods or men; it means the ego's innate, isolated right of defiance, which is punished by the laws of this world. The "positivity" (to use Hegel's term) of external statutes is refuted by the "negativity" of an inner, animated self-certainty: by Pamina's words of decision sung above seven strokes of the strings, a firm, resplendent C major cadence. Death may be the penalty for Pamina's "crime," but why should she fear it as long as death also threatens her irrefutable love, which causes her to recognize and fly to Tamino with a youthfully rash phrase of defiance: "My arms embrace him, *even if it were* my end." Thus death, closer to the girl than the henchmen who seize her, supports rather than suppresses her resistance. – In Pamina's second experience the carefree defiance of death is replaced by weariness unto death: "There will be peace in death" ("So wird Ruh' im Tode sein"). In the G minor aria the voice rises to jagged peaks of pain, then sinks again into the caverns of inwardness, where all traces of certainty and self-pledged right have disappeared. The farewell trio sounds still more desolate, its melodic haste leaving the lovers without even a place to linger in their pain: "You will not evade death" ("Du wirst dem Tode nicht entgehen"). Life, her own and that of her lover, trickles away in the ceaseless eighth notes of the accompaniment. The only way to halt it seems suicide: "Sterben will ich." I want to die.

Mozart did not have much time when he wrote *Die Zauberflöte:* some weeks left to compose, some months to live. His late style creates a fluid alternation of melodic shapes which emerge from and are submerged in one another, yet without thematic contrasts to define or hold back the flow. The music which has overcome all unrest still has no time to linger; this strangely reverses the listener's sense of time. Because the lovely flow of sound glides all too soon to an end, we experience it as if in retrospect—full of blissful regret that it is passing, that it has already passed. Thus in each moment of Pamina's aria, the melodies that move "in an undisturbed stream without any clearly defined motifs" (Jahn) yearn for the phrase which has just faded away, permitting memory to draw delight even from pain. – Nostalgia instilled by music of seamless density appeared earlier in *Così fan tutte:* in the entrancing brevity of the *terzettino,* in many gently concealed transitions between recitative and ensemble and recitative. They are the emblems, inlaid in comedy, of a melancholy but uncomplaining knowledge of transience.

Like the farewell trios of *Così* and *Zauberflöte,* the moments of farewell in Mozart's symphonic music, especially the instrumental concertos, help decipher the language of his late music. Beginning with the piano concertos of 1784, the slow movements end with ever more subtle parting gifts. Their codas often give rise to the overflow of a new melody—which then, in a new light (the last, consoling twilight that falls on things too perfect to be retained) appears as pure cadence, the harmonic sequence of departure.* – In Mozart's final, succinct style, however, these farewell conclusions also become briefer, more taciturn. When the music is all farewell, no threshold should warn the listener before the end and give him time to separate. Therefore the last gesture is compressed, simplified, almost omitted. The orchestral coda of Pamina's G minor aria lasts only four measures. Finally resolving in despair and weariness the diminished seventh chord's tormented question, "Fühlst du nicht der Liebe Sehnen," the orchestra confirms the ultimate answer offered by Pamina's now mute voice: "So wird Ruh' im Tode sein." There will be peace in death. The orchestra bows its head: amen.

---

*We can hear how such pieces remove themselves from us in the briefer and briefer surfacing of their melodic particles in the coda. Thus the slow movement of the A major concerto K.488 sings to a close with the digression of 4+4, 2+2, 2 measures; similarly the D minor K.466 in 4+4, 2+2, 2 (1+1), 2 (1+1); the E-flat major K.482 in 8+8, 4+4, 4; the C minor K.491 in 4+4, 2, 1.

☾

After Pamina's suicide has been put on hold, *Die Zauber-flöte* (despite its avoidance of caesuras within its numbers) has an abrupt caesura. Mozart does not take Pamina's rescue by the Three Boys quite seriously: the childlike cheer of the quartet of four sopranos cannot be the whole story. Fear and grandeur, the dark, bare objectivity of death irrupt with the figured chorale. Soon we will speak of Pamina's third experience, which begins before the gates of fear: of how her offer to die challenges and compels the higher powers to grant her life and love—and how the girl in need of rescue becomes the rescuer.

XVII

For Botho Strauss

MOZART/SCHIKANEDER.   Theatrical genius necessarily involves tracking down, setting free, and exploiting the genius of others. Mozart did this better than anyone. While Sarastro's sublime resignation, Tamino's ingenuous fervor, Pamina's authenticity had to be invented, lured out of the words by Mozart's music, he knew where he could trust Schikaneder entirely and follow him: in the fun and feeling that the poet and actor of magical-farcical-musical comedies gave to Papageno's and Monostatos's heartwarming misery. "Comic spirit" is easy to say, but this kind did not exist before *Die Zauberflöte,* not even in Mozart. The genius that Mozart discovered in his able theater manager and drinking buddy was *Sympathie:* it is no coincidence that this foreign word appears explosively apt in Papageno and Pamina's duet, in the middle of the simplest German words. *Sympathie* is love without possessiveness or blindness, love that does not need to gild or ennoble its object—in short, God's love for those who suffer, and the comedy writer's love for his characters. Mozart was a comedian no less than Schikaneder. As "Männer, welche Liebe fühlen" they could act out Papageno or Monostatos for one another. In 1787, Mozart had his friend Jacquin write in his poetry album that true genius means neither intelligence nor imagination, but love; only now did he completely honor the dictum.

Midsummer moonlight glitters in Monostatos's strange aria, silver as the solo flute's timbre in its highest register. Lunar magic and secrecy have untied the tongue of the villain and slave; not only the music, but every word of his stanzas is full of droll poetry, truer than the hymns of the priests. "Alles fühlt der Liebe Freuden, / Schnäbelt, tändelt, herzet, küsst, / Und ich soll die Liebe meiden, / Weil ein Schwarzer hässlich ist!" The answer: "Drum so will ich, *weil ich lebe,* / Schnäbeln, küssen, zärtlich sein! / Lieber, guter Mond vergebe, / Ein Weisse nahm mich ein!" Schikaneder's following "Weiss ist schön" may show even deeper sympathy for the oppressed than Malcolm X's "Black is beautiful." The final appeal to the celestial goddess, who shines mercifully on everything black, dispels the magical moment with a gesture that hardly could be more tender: "Weiss ist schön, ich muss es küssen. / Mond! verstecke dich dazu! / Sollt' es dich zu sehr verdriessen, / O so mach die Augen zu!"* It is with the gesture of forbearance that Mozart and Schikaneder evoke the miserably abused desires of the Moor. They do not persist

---

*Everything feels love's joys, / Pecks, dallies, caresses, kisses, / And I should avoid love, / Because a black man is ugly . . .

And so, *because I am alive,* / I'll peck, kiss, be tender! / Dear moon, forgive me, / I took to a white woman! . . .

White is beautiful, I must kiss it. / Moon, hide yourself! / If it troubles you too much, / O close your eyes.

in exposing the lust, brutality, self-hatred of his attack on Pamina. The aria's allegro brevity and pianissimo haste, beyond their dreamlike, grotesque, secretive connotations, convey a final, most touching meaning: the heart has its reasons. "That's what we said," the poet and composer tell us after the seventy-second miracle, "and there isn't any more to say. You spectators, you nuisances, the rest is none of your business." O close your eyes.

Papageno's scene with tree and noose profits from Pamina's previous negligible attempt to kill herself. It surprises us, when we least expect it, with the darkest and lightest extremes of the act. What a farewell to the universe: "Weil du böse an mir handelst, / Mir kein schönes Kind zubandelst, / So ist's aus, so sterbe ich."* The birdcatcher's cosmic sulk, his vow to punish the girls of this earth who have run away from him by running away from them, shocks and reconciles us with the self-murderer's duplicity. Papageno embodies suicide's primordial deceit, passing off greed for life as scorn for life, boasting of transcendence while glancing over to see the effect. But he frees it from embarrassment, purifies it in the songs of a candid and childlike ego drive. He babbles out his vainglory in dying—"Pretty girls, think of me!"—instead of covering it up with lies. – Again Mozart and Schikaneder allow *caritas,* heavenly love, to descend in the guise of forbearance, guarding the heartrending dignity with which their protégé draws the curtain over a sadly botched enterprise, his life. "Weil mich nichts zurücke hält, / Gute Nacht, du falsche Welt!" Goodnight, you false world. The G minor melody of acquiescence puts an end to all reproaches and self-reproaches; the time for discussing wrongs or guilt is

---

*Because you treat me wrong, / Provide me with no pretty girl, / That's the end, I'll die.

past—and yet the words add a grain of comic resistance, a last spark of the will to survive: "You false world!"

Schikaneder's sympathy with the clowns of popular farce helped Mozart to add "dignity" to the ranks of his great secularizations. As he turned mercy to pardon, heroic deed to probation, so he recouped Baroque nobility as humane, palpable dignity. Henceforward dignity sides not with gods and princes but with man, for it sides with the most simple of men. Respect for the human being thus was freed of any tie to office, power, or privilege—liberated not by cannons or the guillotine, but through a comedian's drollery on September 30, 1791, in the Freihaus Theater of Vienna.

XVIII

TAMINO. He speaks his most human words *before* he meets the priests of humanity and wisdom. "Paminen retten, ist mir Pflicht." Her rescue—my duty. What wisdom does he need, he who knows so much?

*Pamina's Three Deaths;
or, the Happy Ending*

Three Women Rescuers

"Mozart's greatest work remains *Die Zauberflöte*," said Beethoven. The libretto met his requirement of lofty and trivial absoluteness: "It has to be something moral, uplifting." For him, *Die Zauberflöte* was a promise of *Fidelio*. Humankind, the subject of the singspiel's wondrous tales, is now tangibly embodied in an unrecognized prisoner crouching at Leonore's feet. His powerlessness in the narrow dungeon demands that she break through to the universal. Leonore's need to help her husband is abruptly exalted by the categorical imperative, expanded to embrace the world: "Whoever you are, I shall save you." – True, the public, party-forming rhetoric of *Die Zauberflöte*, opposing *Mensch* to *Unmensch*, man to monster, seems to be superseded by the Kantian, Beethovenian subjectification of the commandment to be human: the night of the *Fidelio* dungeon will not be dispelled by the Order's special sun. The only source of light is the sudden spark of Leonore's decision, which short-circuits the forsaken individuals "you" and "I" with the supreme universal. Yet, unmistakably, the individual's solidarity with everyone who suffers causes a new rupture in the world: Leonore's visionary hope counters Pizarro's tyrannical rage with the same crude symbolism (D minor/E major) with which Sarastro's song of forgiveness refuted the Queen's aria of vengeance. Institutional power is deemed to be, more than ever, a murky conspiracy—and conspiracy against it a radiant anticipated rescue. The Manichean self-righteousness of *Die Zauberflöte* is not mollified in *Fidelio;* rather it is sharpened into a Last Judgment on reality, with the human subject appointed prosecutor and judge. – The act of rescue itself, however, has suddenly grown in sublimity and concreteness, now that it is no longer governed by the claims of the initiates to a monopoly on wisdom and an exclusive franchise as the educators of mankind. Henceforth, rescue springs from the conviction of the heart that says No to injustice; and its deed is resistance. Here, too, Beethoven found prefigured in *Die Zauberflöte* his own surpassing of it.

The rescue of a captive woman from the underworld by a loving man is the oldest plot in opera. Mozart apparently accepted the Orpheus model unquestioningly for his singspiel libretti: Belmonte or Tamino is to free Konstanze or Pamina from imprisonment. But when, before the fearful gates, Orpheus's credo rises with the cheerful confidence of a nursery rhyme—"Wir wandeln durch des Tones Macht / Froh durch des Todes düstre Nacht" (We make our way with music's might / Joyous through death's gloomy night)—it is no longer Tamino but Pamina who leads both the duet and the passage through their trials. Reversing the official myth of a man's initiation by saving a woman, a different, clandestine plot-line asserts itself: how the woman in need of rescue becomes the rescuer. Beethoven's resistance drama speaks aloud the secret of Mozart's fairytale—and thereby changes the basic pattern of opera. The hero of *Fidelio,* which its composer wanted to call *Leonore,* is a woman, not a man. Guided by spontaneity rather than by wisdom or orders from on high, she emulates Pamina, not Tamino. – Leonore celebrates Pamina not merely in word and deed, but also with her voice. Her vocal line floats on a sustained breath that makes the woman on stage toweringly present and alive in body and spirit. The living breath of the dramatic soprano in the realm of danger is our single bold assurance that final salvation is possible, that all the misgivings and tortures of probation will end in approbation. Impatiently, exultingly, Leonore's vocal line extends the great arcs of Pamina's recitatives, those early manifestations of the human subject in the first *Zauberflöte* finale: the *self-discovery* of "Die Wahrheit, die Wahrheit" and the *offer to die* of "Herr, ich bin zwar Verbrecherin." Self–discovery and self–sacrifice thus engender the new song, the new plot. They will overcome the crisis as they fuse into a ritual of rescue, performed by the subject.

Pamina's quest for her own truth and Pamina's passage through three deaths are interwoven throughout the singspiel. They begin together in those arcs of the first finale and end together in the second finale. After the youth's exclamation "Hier sind die Schreckenspforten" (Here are the fearful gates / That threaten me with danger and death), the girl's voice floats down over the dominant seventh chord as if circling, searching—and then sets out resolutely on the final passage: "I will be everywhere / At your side. / I myself will lead you . . ." Pamina's defiance of death, her weariness unto death are succeeded by her third and final meeting with "man's true, best friend." Now that she encounters it with trust and composure, ready to sacrifice herself, death miraculously pledges not the destruction but the survival of the autonomous self. – We could hardly decipher Pamina's last rite of passage (for her words are simple, her mind youthfully shy, her song translucent), if her successor Leonore as well as her predecessor, Goethe's Iphigenie, did not come to her aid: Iphigenie with the graceful, spiritual gift of her speech, Leonore with the expressive thrust of her materialized music. The triad of Iphigenie, Pamina, and Leonore (united by their self-discovery in truth and readiness to die) first placed woman as rescuer in the center of German classicism—which felt that human freedom must remain a fraud if it understood man as subject, but subject solely as a man. These theatrical women taught Goethe, Mozart, Beethoven to admit that autonomy is initiated and sustained not by heroes, but by the weakest of creatures—and that self-determination does not exclude or oppose rescue, but is its very model.

❨ ❨

Crooked Paths to Freedom

The relation between *Iphigenie auf Tauris* and *Fidelio,* however, is rife with perturbation arising from the political and intellectual upheaval between Goethe's final version (1787) and Beethoven's first (1806). The dramatic poem refined its discourse to an even beauty, a "pervading harmony," until words began to sound like music: music that was to banish the demons of prehistory to the chaotic abyss that still gaped. The music drama, on the other hand, exalted its central terms into spiritual beings, inciting "Freiheit," "Gattenliebe," "Hoffnung" (Freedom, Marital Love, Hope) to storm forth like so many demons and break a passage into a future that has begun to petrify anew. Paradoxically, then, Beethoven's work of violence has to do with utopia, and Goethe's work of reconciliation with myth. – The Greek Iphigenia, like no other character in tragedy, was chained to the gods' mythical thirst for blood, their call for human sacrifice; and like no one else she anticipated the birth of the subject out of the threefold union of self-discovery, self-sacrifice, and rescue. With the heroine of *Iphigenia at Aulis,* his last play, Euripides commemorated the earliest leap toward humanity: substitution. From now on, animal sacrifice would replace the slaughter of humans on the idol's altar. But already Euripides' curiosity was focused less on the pity of Artemis than on how Iphigenia succeeded in inducing it—on that precarious first experiment in knitting together autonomy and mercy. The shrewdest of tragedians knew that mere substitution could easily seem like swindling the gods; it resembled too much Odysseus's trick of passing his men off as rams to escape from the cave of man-eating myth. Iphigenia becomes worthy of her rescue when she no longer thinks of escape, but of self-sacrifice: "Death is my portion, so I take / Death upon myself . . . / And all tongues call me / Greece's liberator." Only now does the goddess spirit the girl whose blood she craved from the gory altar into the protective distances of Tauris.

Our topic is the happy ending. Its addictive ingredient (even in commercial comedies and movies) is probably not so much the belief in actual happiness as the hope that human sacrifice can be avoided. Euripides' predecessors used the happy ending; he *desired* it—the first modern. Nietzsche furiously denounced his *deus ex machina* as the precocious draft of an untragic world, already advertising the insipidly rational optimism of modern times. Aristotle seems to contradict this. In the *Poetics* he surprisingly reports that Euripides was attacked by his contemporaries because his heroes' destinies rarely flipped from calamity to success, but instead almost always from fortune to misfortune. Both are true. Euripides needed the deepest abandonment in order to twist it into the highest salvation. And so Iphigenia's path to the happy ending seems oddly crooked: she must not help herself, in order that the gods shall help her. The escape from myth may have been first achieved through shrewdness, through the Odyssean barter, or cheat, of substitution. The rise of the self, however (thus the last of Greek tragedies proclaims), dates from the decision to renounce individual cunning, recognizing oneself in the universal. And yet the gods are subtly duped at Aulis. For Iphigenia sacrifices her life not to Artemis, who demanded it and now spares it, but to the Greek people. The history of the individual advances each time he "freely" adjusts, indeed assimilates to the ascendant power of the day, in order to untangle himself from the power in decline—in due course from myth, from religion, and finally from the collective. – Tragedy makes itself the accomplice of this process, first by turning the offer to die (which mediates self-discovery with rescue) from a miraculous exception into a protective ritual; then by rationalizing the success of that ritual into the strategy of a repeatable action; finally, by publicizing the moves of that strategy on the stage, as a standard plot. Euripides teaches the renunciation of calculation as a calculated survival technique for the powerless, the renunciation of cleverness as the safest way to outwit the powerful.

That is why Nietzsche called his tragedies deceptions, mere comedies in disguise—indeed worse than comedies, in which deception and disguise work openly toward a happy end. Both enlightened and blinded by his hatred for the commercial savvy of emancipation, Nietzsche saw the gods' mercy, longed for by the author and brought about by the protagonist, as nothing but the sweaty ascent of economic man. Euripides' hero, "after being sufficiently lacerated by fate, reaped his well-earned reward in a profitable marriage or godlike honors." The causal linkage of toil and profit would indeed bring us into the closed New Comedy world of citizens and slaves, where shrewdness, having escaped the bondage of myth, religion, and collectivity, holds sway without force: as the cunning of each individual who fights through to his own happiness, and as the cunning of the whole, discreetly represented by the author, who combines the opposing energies of individuals into a happy outcome. Nietzsche's hatred is possibly rooted in the snobbish repugnance of the minister's son and the scholar, to whom the merchant still smells like the slave he had been until he bought his freedom. Yet in his scorn for comedy as the genre of the common (and the commoners), in his glorification of tragedy as the genre of the noble (and the nobility), the prophet of the Superman stands less alone than he wishes. It was precisely the Euripidean Aristotle and his parroting disciples (right down to Baroque simpletons like Opitz) who stuck to the idea of the "higher" dramatic form—not because they believed in gods and destiny, but because they loathed to seek the impulse and goal of human behavior in something so gross as self-preservation, rather than in domination and self-immolating pride. – Even Euripides allowed his propounding of autonomy to be curtailed by the limits of tragedy's aristocratic ethics. In his early and middle plays, the gods make sure that the tortured individual's cunning (which is always women's cunning: Electra's, Iphigenia's, Hecuba's) ends in extreme peril or bloody catastrophe. Neither will the fatherland, to which Iphigenia transfers her loyalty in his last tragedy, rescue the individual. Patriotism cannot do without human sacrifice; therefore its rule does not abolish, but rather inherits murderous domination mythic or divine.*

At the moment when Iphigenia, calculating in her innocence, offers her life to the goddess but gives it to the fa-

---

*Only Falstaff, the spirit of comedy in open uprising against tragedy, will eventually muster the courage to be a coward and refuse to die for the fatherland. Distinguishing between *dulce* and *decorum,* he prefers life to honor. Cast aground on the field of honor, he chooses the most brilliant disguise, the most profound cunning: instead of dying, he pretends to be dead.

therland, the humans are probably deceiving themselves even more than they do the gods. It was during the Peloponnesian War that Euripides wrote the four extant or partly extant tragedies of his which treat of patriotic self-sacrifice. In each of them, to ensure victory the gods and the people demand the blood not of the hero, king, or general, but of his defenseless child. The child immolates itself and in exchange is rescued—or turned into a friendly spring or a twinkling star. But is Euripides' apotheosis of Macaria, Menoeceus, the daughters of Erechtheus, Iphigenia more honest or truthful than media drumbeating for totalitarian ruling gangs, which drives glory-addicted adolescents to the front line even when final defeat is imminent? – The sacrifice itself, and even more the freedom of the one who freely sacrifices himself, deserve acute suspicion. If Iphigenia did not call for her own death, she would still be killed. The inflated paean that praises and buries her, "Here she departs, / The great destroyer / Of the enemy's city," gives her her due less than does Adorno's reticent suggestion: "The time-honored belief in sacrifice is perhaps but a drilled-in pattern, by which the oppressed do themselves the same injustice that has been done to them, in order to be able to bear it." – The chorus's final hymn to the Hellenic nation and against the barbarians in the east may even have had a pacific, utopian undertone when Euripides wrote it; for the eighty-year-old was tormented by the annihilating struggle between Hellenes, and nostalgic for their unanimity gained and lost during the Persian Wars. In any case, the price of nationwide peace must be paid by the most innocent of Greek women—not by Agamemnon or Achilles, who would joyfully strangle each other rather than combat the barbarians, even as they set sail to murder them together.

"I Shall Unchain You"

Goethe's heroine however refuses to use deceit, as well as violence, against the barbarians. That in no way follows from the poet's choice of Iphigenia at Tauris, rather than at Aulis, for his subject. From this same story (the adventurous escape of three Greeks from the land of the barbarians) Euripides drew an action full of cunning and national pride, while Goethe aims at the opposite: the praise of truth and humanity. His twofold protest against his model is a single decision, the *raison d'être* of his drama. – The more a man untangles himself from his last particular tie—to his nation—the greater is his need to hold on to the value that seems removed from particularity, from all inequality of belief, race, or power: the proscription against deceit, the prescription for truth. The vow of truthfulness is the earliest and yet mildest coercion of our species; we invented speech by swearing each individual to a consensus about the meaning of words, that they are to say what is, not what is not. Goethe's Iphigenie recapitulates this first step of the human race as the last step toward humanity—which means the self-confirmation as well as the self-disarmament of the subject as it becomes free and therefore unbridled. To achieve the socialization of such free people, "truth" must embrace both of its senses: the attainment of one's inmost identity, and the surrender of one's external nonidentity, cunning and lies. The great confessions of Iphigenie, Pamina, Leonore advertise by their artistic persuasion that attaining and surrendering the self are inseparable and must happen simultaneously. In the moment of their fusion into one dramatic gesture, they become legible as self-discovery and self-sacrifice. This new gesture of truth, however, is unmistakably a quotation of the old gesture of sacrifice.

The Classical enterprise could easily be derided for pinning its hopes on truth at the outset of a bourgeois era that prized Odyssean traits. It further could be accused of supporting that parochial German naivety or hypocrisy which persisted in praising the "upright" craftsman and the "honest" merchant right into the era of Krupp and the stock market speculators—and preached "good faith" and "sincerity" ("Treu' und Redlichkeit") as the cardinal virtues of subordinates. And yet truth was never less a mere moral cliché or logical tautology than during the Classical period. In that brief flash of light between 1780 and 1800, truth appeared as the force into which sacrifice, the regulator of all earlier communal living, was to be absorbed, supplanting timelessly endured oppression with a newly conceived freedom. – This is why in the crisis of Goethe's *Iphigenie* (V, 3) the human history of sacrifice is recapitulated with a driving insistence. An order to commit holy murder is confronted by the refusal to do so. The clash is followed by the riskiest of decisions—to renounce the life-saving cunning that the individual had used to escape mythical threat: "a pure soul does not need it." The drama steps out of a past that it has had to banish to the present and future of utopian modernity. Only now can Iphigenie speak her twofold challenge to Thoas: words that seek a world without deception, but also without a helpless re-lapse into servitude to monsters, to gods, to one's own race and nation: "Glorify truth through me!" and: "Then kill me first!" Quoted but transmuted, this sacrificial gesture ends the age of sacrifice. By uniting self-discovery with self-sacrifice, Iphigenie establishes the paradigmatic plot of the Classical period: the woman in need of rescue becomes the rescuer. Orestes, who was supposed to lead his captive sister from the underworld of the barbarians back to the light of Greece, now addresses her with a thanksgiving formerly reserved for the gods: "Da alle Rettung auf der weiten Erde / Verloren schien, gibst du uns alles wieder." When all rescue on the wide earth seemed lost, you restore everything to us.

Iphigenie auf Tauris requires a long scene of glorious elo-quence for what transpires in *Fidelio* with eschatological haste. The confessional revelation of the truth and the offer to die are voiced in the same words (confirming Aristotle's proposal that *anagnorisis* and *peripeteia* might be identical in essence). The words need only four notes in the boldest modulation, from D to B-flat: "Töt erst sein Weib!"—First kill his wife! Leonore throws off her disguise, that most ambiguous instrument of theatrical salvation, symbolizing at once comic self-preservation and tragic self-extinction, cunning and immersion in death. She now stands defense-less and invincible in her guilelessness. Hardly a minute later the tidings of rescue ring out, again in the same heart-piercing modulatory leap from the tonal realm of G to that of E-flat: the trumpet signal. – The power of this minute has been gathering for millennia. It concentrates all the hope and experience that struggled out of the archaic slaughter-house ooze to inform Iphigenie's, Pamina's, Leonore's re-sistance in truth, their liberation won and attested by the subject. Beethoven paid his debt to Pamina by celebrating her with the most gripping paraphrase of the first Classical period given by the second. He augmented Pamina's rescue theme "Ich selbsten führe dich" (I myself shall lead you) into the unstoppable C major ascent of Leonore's voice, surging onward and upward to an ecstatic coloratura of promise and determination: "Gewiss, ich löse deine Ketten, / Ich will, du Armer, dich befrein." Truly, I shall unchain you. Again, *Fidelio* only reveals a secret from *Die Zauberflöte*—but what a secret, what a revelation.

Readings XIX–XXVII

XIX

PROBATION AND REWARD. The endlessly blissful moment in Mozart when mercy bowed down to autonomy   <rem
lasted only a moment. It was extinguished by the dynam-
ics of bourgeois emancipation, which loathed to owe anything to the will of gods and princes and hastily obliterated
all reminders of aid or bounty from above. Mozart did not
innocently suffer this process: he contributed to it with his
last opera.

   Late in June 1791 he finished composing the first act of
Die Zauberflöte, which concludes in mercy; but mercy had
come into disrepute throughout Europe. On June 6, the
Constituent Assembly in Paris had denounced and abolished the king's right to grant amnesty, calling it an "arbitrary instrument of princely favoritism." In the debate it
was claimed that mercy, as a single, rationally unjustifiable
act of favor, infringed the principle of equality before
the law and was therefore an "injustice, an assault on society." Pétion, the chief spokesman for the radicals, shared
Bentham's (Beccaria's, Kant's) suspicion: "Each act of amnesty gives the tyrant a reputation for lenience and helps to
conceal the cruelty of the laws." From that he derived the
tenet which mortally wounded late absolutism and its ideology of *clemenza:* "Justice is the clemency of nations!"
(Pétion died two years later of starvation as he fled the
revolutionary tribunal; his corpse was found in the woods,
gnawed by beasts of prey.) – Sarastro revokes his decree of
amnesty toward Pamina and Tamino when he orders:
"Lead these two strangers into our Temple of Trials." Act
II can now begin. In it, autonomy is not to be crowned by
mercy; instead, probation shall earn its own reward. Equal
pay for equal toil becomes the bourgeois model of justice.*

*Beccaria's *Dei delitti e delle pene* demands this kind of rationality:
penalties proportionate to each other and to the crimes (considered as

In *Le nozze di Figaro* Mozart had not only lavishly fulfilled the bourgeois' deepest wish, that probation be followed by a just (that is, proportionate and unfailing) reward, but he also admitted such longing to his earthly paradise. There, autonomy dwells peaceably with mercy: the pursuit of happiness is topped off by forgiveness, the wily intrigue resolved by the wonderfully generous outcome. *Die Zauberflöte,* on the other hand, attempts to secularize—indeed to calculate—the blessing that exceeds all merit (and therefore falls under the suspicion of sharing in favoritism and arbitrariness). Thus Sarastro's clemency, which blessed Pamina's self-discovery in the first act, is to be paid out to Tamino, after the intermission, as the due recompense for his labors. – Sarastro's tone in opening the second act is mixed. He still sounds like the enlightened imperial bureaucrat keeping patronizing watch over the prosperity of trade and industry—as well as the chief executive, our contemporary, gratified to introduce a talented newcomer of noble background to his board of directors: "Tamino, a prince, twenty years of age, strives in his virtuous heart for an object that we all must secure by our industrious efforts." Tamino's career has begun; he will rise by his exertions and through his connections (those final, shabbily up-to-date secularizations of autonomy and mercy).

In the first act, the bourgeois work ethic broke through only once, in the key lines signaling Tamino's conversion to the world of achievement and advancement. Arriving in

---

injuries to society). Hence arose the obsession of the Enlightenment (Mercier, Bentham), unique in legal history, to couple a system of rewards with the system of punishment. Only when merit and reward (or injury and damages paid) become calculably identical in size and value has the aristocratic ethic of merit been supplanted by bourgeois equity, functioning as a system of exchange.

the outer court of the Empire of the Sun, he wonders, "Is this the seat of the gods?" But it was not the threefold dedication to "Reason," "Nature," and "Wisdom" on the three temple facades that fascinated him; rather, it was work: the craftsmanship of their construction. "The gates and columns show / That cleverness and work and the arts dwell here. / Where diligence holds sway and idleness recedes, / Vice becomes powerless." Each monastic or secular order emits a particular scent to attract novices. The Priests of Wisdom lure the "Javonese" prince not with pious incense or scholarly mustiness, but with the sweat of *homo oeconomicus,* which he is inhaling for the first time. Kierkegaard, despiser of the bourgeoisie, noted that Tamino's new moral taste is thoroughly unmusical, indeed anti-musical. Tamino in fact keeps silent ("schweigt still") so he need not sing along with the clichés of his teachers. Of all the solo parts, he alone has no solo of his own in the second act. Even more blatantly, of the five arias in that act, one is sung by Pamina and three are sung to her (by Monostatos, the Queen, and Sarastro). The fifth, however, the *Mädchen oder Weibchen* song, is not struck up by Papageno until his grumpy guardian of a prince has retired into the wings.

Note. If we wish to learn how probation and reward may grow into great, serious music, bursting all the bonds of proportion by their excess, we must listen to the dungeon act of *Fidelio.* There, for a brief while, the bourgeois exchanges his work ethic for the ethic of liberation (although Rocco, whenever his assistant sings of freedom, quickly reminds him to keep digging). The bourgeois becomes hero and demigod in the herculean enterprise of sweeping the primeval monster of tyranny off the face of the earth. – It has been reported, though, that Wilhelmine Schröder-

Devrient, singing Leonore for the first time, faltered and collapsed at the trumpet signal. The role proved to be one of unique, heroic overexertion.

XX

YOU ARE MINE. The question that Beaumarchais' comedy *Figaro* extracted from the foundations of tragedy was whether one man may dominate another. The raging of the Count in his servants' quarters makes his privilege thematic and thus questionable. With the change in genre, domination loses its self-evidence as a convention, which had enabled it, ever since Aeschylus, to sustain the tragic world of noble, aristocratic sublimity and terror. The ridicule that hoped to prove fatal to domination on the stage in *Figaro* allowed it to return to the serious theater (in nineteenth-century history plays and opera) only as melodrama—which depends on the pact between author and audience to overlook the ridiculous. Hebbel's enterprise as a dramatist, the last great attempt at tragedy, was revealed by Nestroy in all its deep, devastating absurdity. Because the sovereign's greatness has lost its plausibility, Holofernes must exhibit greatness as a personal attribute, as a quasi-pathological peculiarity of his character. "Who's the stronger, me or me?" he roars in Nestroy's pastiche. (Until Brecht's *Die Massnahme,* Genet's *Le balcon,* there will be no truly political drama in Europe; for everyone, except for those freaks Kleist and Büchner, convince themselves that, after *Figaro* and 1789, domination has vanished not only from the stage, but from the civilized world.)

The true question that Hebbel's tragedy *Judith* extracted from comedy (reversing the direction) is whether one person may *own* another. New Comedy recovered from the abolition of slavery (which was the foundation of

Menander's and Plautus's little middle-class world) with Molière. He chose for his basic situation what was left of slavery: the middle-class husband's conviction that he is his wife's proprietor. Of all comedy writers, he found the most earnest disciples; they made it clear that there would be no more joking about that claim. The recognition that ownership, not domination, is the key relationship between man and woman remained the insight of *Herodes und Mariamne, Gyges und sein Ring,* and indeed *Die Nibelungen*. With this insight Hebbel, who thought he was restoring tragedy, anticipated Ibsen's and even Wedekind's bourgeois drama (while the work he declared a *drame bourgeois, Maria Magdalene,* turned into a traditional piece along the lines of Lessing and Schiller). – More wickedly than any other, the play of Lulu scratches at one human's right to possess another human. It is as if in 1893, a full century after Beaumarchais, Wedekind wanted to test whether his modern horror tragedy, *Schauertragödie,* could make property impossible in life by dragging it on the stage, as the older comedy had done to domination. Wedekind was a non-Communist. He ended his question not with an exclamation point, but with a question mark—whose twists and turns he may have thought better suited to describe the paths of history.

XXI

NIHIL HUMANUM. The wise and observant Hermann Abert noted how in two instances Mozart sets surprise to music. The world does not resist the shock with agitation and revolt; petrified, it cracks. When Cherubino is discovered in the armchair, "there is no sound of impulsive surprise, no reaction of the mind or will. Everybody seems to be dazed, and therefore the machinery keeps on running automatically along its old track, but finally stops because its propulsion is removed. The strings simply get stuck at Basilio's theme, turning it aimlessly this way and that; deep down in the bassoons, and later in the clarinets as well, the same motif stirs, but already lethargic, unwieldy, as if swollen; one of the oboes and the two horns, for their part, from the beginning remain in mysterious rigidification in a threefold octave on the dominant. The dominant harmony shows its vigor for a while, but then it too gives way, and finally the whole clockwork stops at a general pause." The other instance is when Masetto steps out of the garden pavilion to confront Giovanni: "No eruption in the orchestra, no change in beat or tempo, not even a *forte,* but rather the same rigid petrification of one single motif . . . The surprise is expressed not in any kind of exaltation but in a general paralysis." We are told how unusual Mozart's procedure was: "Hardly any other contemporary, let alone subsequent, composer would have resisted a *fortissimo* orchestral outburst on a dissonance."

Abert does not mention two passages of surprise music that work with broader strokes but the same perception: in the last *Figaro* finale, after the Countess has unmasked herself, and in the sextet from *Don Giovanni,* when Leporello is unmasked. By reiterating one short staccato figuration that seems to circle endlessly without moving from the spot, the violins bring time to a halt, in the eighth-note scales of the finale and in the repeated sixteenth notes of the sextet. Above them we hear the interrupted chords (*sotto voce* between general pauses) of the ensemble, huddling together as a chorus, as if the event had not only taken away the breath of its witnesses but also erased their faces. In Mozart's operas, surprise appears with life-threatening strangeness; for the luminous, variegated flow of time, which has abruptly stopped, is the vital element of his characters. Indeed, we would not be able to recognize the unique way in which the stream of time flows through Mozart's creatures and nourishes them, if he himself did not dam it at these moments—and strand us, as he does them, at the end of his world. The characters who have suddenly faced the nothingness of their wits and lives, first respond by stammering, whispering "O cielo!" in *Figaro,* "Dei!" in *Don Giovanni.* Amazement has fractured their beautiful, lovingly self-protected human shape, which like Narcissus had knelt over the inmost mirror of the soul, out of which perfectly shaped song surged as a reflection of their completeness.

Now they stand upon the stage literally dumbfounded, for the source of their song has drained away; they stand literally shattered, for the outline of their person has broken up. But out of those general pauses, the gaps in their breathing and in their world, do they hear any answer from the one they have called on—"Heaven" or "God"?

From this point the dispute whether Mozart's music is religious or irreligious should be reassessed. The call of the ensemble turned chorus by its surprise rises from the furthest edge of immanence; but it reaches no beyond, nothing radically other. It says that for Mozart the limits of multitudinous individuality, of time as the medium of sensation and sensuality, were also the end of things conceivable and true. "O cielo!" and "Dei!" paradoxically attest that everything nonhuman was alien to him. (If the limitations and failures of the human are, as many believe, the best evidence of the divine, then the gods are man's weakest invention: hallucinations of his loss of consciousness, stand-ins for his impotence. Mozart's strongest character is the blasphemer. And yet when Giovanni confronts the Stone Guest, he betrays his own pathology: deafness and blindness to surprise.)

XXII

BOURGEOIS ET GENTILHOMME. In the great treatise that is the preface to his tearful "domestic tragedy" *Eugénie,* Beaumarchais followed Diderot's example in combating the old aesthetic rule of decorum, which separated tragedy and comedy according to the social standing of their characters: "The real empathy of the heart, the true connection, goes from man to man, not from man to prince. The splendor of rank in no way increases my compassion for tragic characters, but on the contrary hinders it. The closer the suffering man's estate is to mine, the more fiercely his misfortune takes hold in my soul." – The sharp disparity of tone, mood, and dramatic structure between *Eugénie* and *Le mariage de Figaro* has kept scholarly criticism from discovering how their respective ventures are linked: how they prove themselves contemporaries precisely by their difference. As Beaumarchais escorts the bourgeois into tragedy in *Eugénie,* so in *Figaro* he lures the nobleman into the servants' quarters, into the dusky park, where the jurisdiction of comedy holds sway with malicious disrespect: two stratagems of literature for shaking up the hierarchies of life.

The comedy of the closed form from Menander to Molière is downright obsessed with excluding from its universe anything alien to the bourgeois, his truths and trappings. It will not do to charge this seclusion solely to the middle class and overlook the disgraceful existence of laws well into the nineteenth century (in Prussia for example) that

barred the commoner from acquiring land and the nobleman from the disreputable exercise of a trade or from mar-
rying a commoner's daughter. – And yet it is equally
inaccurate to simplify the craftsman's or merchant's obdu-
rate insistence on social homogeneity in life and on the
stage as something merely imposed on him from above (to
which he then reacted as a true bourgeois, adapting out-
wardly while placating himself with inner defiance: "If
they won't let me, then I don't want to!"). There is a
deeper motive for his avoiding tragedy and seizing comedy
for himself. The immanence of his own surveyable world
was what his day's work strove for, in order to protect his
earnings from the depredations of nature and the ruling
class. The immanence of a reasonable and predictable life
together should also be depicted in his art, through which
he could share with his own kind his present experiences
and his utopian aims.*

Hence the refusal to bring nobles (and gods) onto the
comic stage—immanence—was always ambiguous: on the
one hand the humble confirmation that there were two dis-
tinct worlds, on the other hand the secret dream that there
could be one truly homogeneous world of equals. Because
the rule of decorum thus fused opportunism with hope,
apologetic with utopian impulses, because the division of
the genres grew not out of an autonomous artistic will but
out of a social reflex of the middle-class dramatist—therefore the rule, while it was imposed on aesthetics for two
thousand years, never could be justified totally and purely

*The tautology of such keeping to oneself, saying only what is al-
ready known, has been routinely called the "realism" of comedy. And
yet realism in literature does not emerge until knowledge of the real
world becomes inseparable from disgust and anxiety at its relentless reification—that is, after the decline of European comedy (brought about
by reification).

through aesthetics. "Comedy," wrote Opitz in 1624, "is made up of simple ways, simple people; it speaks of weddings, carousing, games, servant's tricks and wiles, boastful soldiers, lovers' wooing, the folly of youth, the avarice of age, pandering and such things that happen daily among common people." Instead of offering a rationale for the genre, Opitz gives only an inventory of its Greek and Roman stock of characters and plots. But this feeble procedure is followed the more promptly and absolutely with the restrictive law of genres: "Hence, those writers of comedies today err greatly when they introduce emperors and potentates, for that is diametrically opposed to the rules of comedy."

Beaumarchais does not attempt in *Le mariage de Figaro* to escape into Aristophanean or Shakespearean expanses; rather, he transgresses the rule of decorum on its own closed territory: New Comedy. Count Almaviva was born a high aristocrat and owes his post as the Chief Justice of Andalusia to no merit other than his birth—which turns him into a caricature of gods and princes, who govern and judge by virtue of the sheer, irreducible fact of their existence. He is a "potentate." As a ruler, whose own plot is tragedy, he wants to prevail in comedy through his superior being rather than through competition with his fellow humans; that is *his* aberration "diametrically opposed to the rules of comedy." *Le mariage de Figaro* thematizes domination as the anathematized nontheme of New Comedy. For New Comedy had always feared that the intrusion of dominance would disrupt first the dialectic clockwork of cunning in its plot and then the seamless exchange of repartee in its dialogue. (As tragedy's tirades and stichomyths imitate a duel between rival aristocrats, so comedy's dialogue is modeled on exchange in a community of equals.) But *Le mariage de Figaro* disarms such fear in a unique way: with the very dialectic of its plot, the very wit of its dialogue, it dispels the Count's presumption of being unequal, of standing above all exchange and competition; it heals the ruler's image of himself as if it were a disorder of the brain and behavior. And so this one comedy triumphs both over the rules of class on stage and over the ruling class in life. – But is Beaumarchais actually so unique a transgressor? Did all other New Comedy writers stick to the rules? Molière himself created no less than two two-class plots (leaving *Dom Juan* and *Amphitryon* temporarily aside): *Georges Dandin* and *Le bourgeois gentilhomme*. Let us measure them by the rule, in order to measure the rule by them.

The stories of the commoners Dandin and Jourdain are based on a very odd, indeed inverted kind of dramaturgy. In a normal specimen of New Comedy the immoderation and irrationality of a deviant are ground down by a moderate and reasonable bourgeois community, working through the machinery of intrigue. Thus the "character" of the miser from Euclio to Harpagon, or of the misanthrope from Cnemon to Alceste, is mocked and punished, perhaps corrected, according to the rude judgment of Menander: "O thrice unlucky man, / How mightily arrogant are you, vain fool!" *(epitrepontes)*. But Dandin's and Jourdain's stories do not deal with the arrogance of a vice-ridden bourgeois, swaggering within the bounds of comic decorum, who invariably is defeated by the homogeneity of the middle, that is, of middle-class life and views. Instead, without being asked, comedy this time sets out to defend not the bourgeoisie but the nobility—hardly the shabby noblemen on stage but rather the idea of rank itself, the inviolability of inborn privilege. Not the deviant within his own class but the intruder into an alien class is the protagonist who is indicted and mocked in both of Molière's rule-offending comedies. – Dandin and Jourdain are mirror opposites of Almaviva. These intruders wish to transgress class lines from below rather than from above. Their plays are not about a count among commoners, but about a commoner among country squires or counts. Hence the opposing lessons of these plays: the defeat of the upstart reinforces instead of questions the social hierarchy. If *Le mariage de Figaro* is the most critical comedy, then *Georges Dandin* and *Le bourgeois gentilhomme* are the most apologetic: as the former tries to disrupt, so the latter two attempt to ossify the existing order—that form of society that was almost literally copied by the form of comedy.*

The dazzling, keen exuberance of the ending of Beaumarchais' *Figaro* comes from the victory over tragedy: the fallen potentate is no longer granted its time-honored grandeur. The black madness of the conclusions of Molière's Dandin and Jourdain plays, on the contrary, comes from respect for tragedy, whose consolation must not be granted to the humiliated bourgeois, not even in the agony of his misfortune. – Of Molière's protagonists, only one crosses the boundary between the classes from above, not below, much like Beaumarchais' Count—and in utter dislocation he dances, stilt-walks, staggers, falls between comedy and tragedy. Like Almaviva, Dom Juan combs the realm of commoners not for the bourgeois but for the bourgeoise. He approaches women with the will to dominate; with each embrace he ravishes humanity. Molière, however, does not yet know about Beaumarchais' comic

---

*An experiment can show how totally and aggressively *Figaro* reverses the entire structure and the moral of *George Dandin*. Imagine that Beaumarchais had written his play to mock the bourgeois daughter who wanted to marry a count. At the center we would then have the unthinkable line "Rosine, tu l'as voulu!"—That's what you wanted.

community, which, as humanity writ large, will wrest from the ruler his power to rule, thus punishing and redeeming him. In the most skewed of dramatic conclusions, therefore, Molière's Juan is overtaken not by human derision and cunning, but by divine vengeance—not because he has abused defenseless women but because he has blasphemed against the all-powerful fathers, his own as well as the heavenly one. *Dom Juan* extends its plot into three classes: the hero's malevolent encroachment into the bourgeois world is grossly imitated by heaven's malicious attempt to seize the hero. The entrance of the vengeful god violates the rule of decorum far more brutally than did the entrance of the *grand seigneur*. This monstrosity of a comedy offers negative proof of the real purpose of that rule: less to protect the aristocrats' ideal dignity in all drama than to secure the commoners' proprietary hold on comedy. For as soon as the Stone Guest appears, Dom Juan's victims (Opitz's "common people") are forgotten as if they had never existed. For once, the protagonist's defeat is not their triumph; and, to add insult to injury, their oppressor snatches the part of the victim from them.

Dom Juan's destruction by the fathers attains its full historical stature only later, when the bourgeois must choose for himself between his freedom as a man and his authority as a father. Giovanni's revolt against the fathers then gives the nobleman a claim to that humanity which his predecessor and he himself had trampled underfoot. The middle classes now shrink from what they might only now accomplish: to make the world in their hopeful image of interplay among equals. But the potentate who threatened to destroy that interplay now takes up its challenge and speaks for it until his very end, the end of great European comedy. That is why Giovanni has more strength and grandeur than Almaviva—and that is why he does not wholly gain them until he atones for his crime against *humanitas* with a revolt against *auctoritas,* and perishes. – Through their parallels and divergences, *Le nozze di Figaro* and *Don Giovanni* jointly share in the endgame of the genres. Even as their irregular two-class or three-class plots turn on domestication or execution of the ruling-class hero, their song realizes class-transcending humanity. *Figaro,* the last comedy, and *Don Giovanni,* the end of comedy, break the bourgeois limitations of two thousand years of comedy; and the final, lethal splendor of their achievement stands against the failure of the *drame bourgeois.* That programmatic fusion of genres and classes solemnly cancels the rule of decorum in the name of hu-mankind—and yet it can never create true and real human-ity on stage. For the heroes of bourgeois tragedy, from Lessing's Odoardo Galotti to Hebbel's Master Anton, are already exercising a new kind of rule. They are (through no merit other than their birth) fathers rather than humans: potentates.

XXIII

INCOGNITO. "Jupiter, qui sans doute en plaisirs se con-naît, / Sait descendre du haut de sa gloire suprème; / Et pour entrer en tout ce qui lui plaît / Il sort tout à fait de lui-même."* Mercury heralds it at once in the prologue: *Amphitryon* is going to be a three-class tale about gods, masters, and servants, revoking *Dom Juan* with a feast of joyous reconciliation. We are assured of this not only by the play's golden rhythms and rhymes—shimmering with irony, sparkling with parody—which divest the gods of their dignity and power; the fable itself has even more con-

---

*Jupiter, who certainly is an expert in pleasures, / Knows how to descend from the heights of his glory; / And to enter all that pleases him, / He goes completely outside himself.

ciliatory wit than the language. When Jupiter, cloaked in human flesh, slips between the legs of a woman, he exposes himself in more than one sense. Where he is heading, the god of gods now does not have an inch on her husband. The play of erotic mishap (in its lasciviousness as limpid as the Aegean, in its distress as radiant as southern skies) closes the gap between gods and men by transmuting them, confusing them in their neo-heathen entwinement. The myth of the god who misuses his power and sires the demigod is itself transmuted into the utopia of the ruler who renounces power and abdicates into the human condition.

Pastiche is able to bring about what all the lofty examples of absolutist *clemenza* fail to: a truce between sovereignty and humanity. Molière prematurely accomplished this in the tirades of Jupiter, as did Offenbach belatedly in the couplets of Pluto in *Orphée,* of the Viceroy in *Périchole,* who sing the ecstasies of roving incognito. The ruler who voluntarily becomes the lover, the lover who throws off like restrictive garments the identity he has obtained through rule—might not the heavenly visitor of yore, who squandered his dominion over the world, be a model today and tomorrow of an earthly resident who would lovingly share rather than solitarily rule his planet? "Il sort tout à fait de lui-même." In *Amphitryon* happiness means stepping outside oneself, that selfhood that oppresses others and itself. Molière has written plays more clever, important, trenchant; never did he write anything more beautiful.

XXIV

UND BIST DU NICHT WILLIG. The difficulty of describing Giovanni: one may as well try to draw the outline of a rapidly flowing stream. Giovanni has no character;

that is why he is reviled, that is what he boasts about. –
Another explanation: because he is body, not mind, we
cannot get him into our heads. The impossibility of com-

prehending Giovanni: the blame should not fall on him,
but on the lifeless, narrow incomprehension in most of
Western comprehension.

One of Mozart's contemporaries, not yet inhibited by any
tradition of admiration or prettification, saw Giovanni's
character—lack of character—as no one today dares to see
it: "He is the craziest, most nonsensical malformation of an
errant Spanish fantasy. A most lewd, base, nefarious fellow, whose life is an unbroken series of infamies, murders,
and seductions of innocents. A hypocrite and religious
scoffer, an abject rake, a crafty deceiver, a double-dealer
and a fop, the most treacherous, cruel *beast,* a villain without conscience or honor. He commits the greatest atroci-
ties as coolly as if he were drinking up a glass of water; he
stabs a man as if he were going to a dance, seduces and betrays female virtue as if he were taking a pinch of snuff.
And all these abominations amuse him, he thinks all these
bestialities a lot of fun" (Schink, *Dramaturgische Monate,*
1790). If the *dramatis persona* were just the sum of his views
and deeds and not also the signature of history, his cas-
tigator would be irrefutably right.

One can conclude from this that "divine art ought never
debase itself to become the foil of such a scandalous subject" (Beethoven). Or one can toss Beethoven onto the
same heap with Schink and, praising Giovanni's sensual
and expressive vigor, brand both of them as bigots. There
is only one thing the critic may not do: spiritualize the pro-
fligate in order to gratify his own bigotry. The opera's first
scene has been interpreted thus: "A rape would totally
contradict Giovanni's nature and principles. His desire

arises from the infinite longing of his senses, it idealizes the respective victim. Facing him, woman feels herself lifted above reality . . ." (Walter Felsenstein, 1960). The author's prudery (his warmed-over Victorianism calling itself social realism) dribbles from the compressed lips of a State Opera general manager who has chewed all lofty notions of yore into an eclectic mush: "nature," "principles," "infinite longing." – But as little as Giovanni "idealizes" his "victims" ("pur che porti la gonnella": as long as she's in a skirt, he does with her—you know what), he nonetheless has become the victim of such idealizations. For their sake, the famous opera director neglected to read his libretto and his score.

113

According to da Ponte, Giovanni approaches both Anna and Zerlina first with seduction (bluntly speaking, with a disguise and a false promise of marriage) and finishes with unsuccessful rape. We may doubt whether Anna's *accompagnato* vision of that burning black night of prologue gives an accurate report of the outcome of the erotic struggle—but not that he attempted, and she sought to resist, violence. Likewise, if Mozart pinched the bottom of the Zerlina singer to coerce the proper scream from the wings in the ballroom finale, then no doubt Giovanni was supposed to apply a ruder pressure before the victim of assault (neither unprepared nor overanxious) screamed and fled. – I am not trying to devise a "concept" for a novel production in which Giovanni acts like a cheap cad, darting out from behind some fairground bushes. But we must open our eyes to the story and its protagonist, to open our ears to the unprecedented vocal character (fusing mellifluence and brutality) of the *Kavalierbariton* who is no cavalier. We are trying to get at the crux of the Giovanni role: the unity of seduction and violence.

To attribute seduction to Mozart and da Ponte's hero and deny him violence would be to castrate him, to cut him off from his historical source and therefore from his mythical power. Don Juan's tale stems from the only myth which could thrive in modern times: that of the man who is on familiar terms with the devil. He learns from the alchemist of Hell how to amalgamate seduction with violence. In damnation's theo-anthropology, seduction stands for the rebellion of the flesh; violence, for the fall from God. To be sure, the Don Juan legend has two separable origins: the story of the man addicted to women (*Il dissoluto punito* is the true title of da Ponte's libretto) and the story of the blasphemer (*Il convitato di pietra* was da Ponte's model, whose model in turn was *L'athée foudroyé*). How urgently they need each other is shown by the fact that the connection between seduction and violence first appeared in the atheist strain of the fable, but could reach its full cogency and impact only in the womanizer strain. The one tale waited for the other; only together could they become the legend of deicide through earthly pleasure, the myth of an age that put an end to myth.

The Ingolstadt Jesuit drama about Duke Leontius (1615) tells how the young blasphemer speaks abusively to a skull on the roadside and, scoffing at the immortality of the soul, invites it to dinner. Machiavel, the Duke's tutor, takes part in the feast; he leaves the victim of his evil teachings only when the guest drags his host down to hell. Baroque mainstream opinion held Machiavelli to be the devil's ambassador on earth, the great counselor and corrupter of the human race in matters of seduction and violence. His fatal, inexplicable entrance releases the synthesis of the Don Juan material. – The real Machiavelli wrote *Il Principe* for the use of one particular prince, who was supposed to strengthen his territories from within, end the inter-city wars in Italy, and drive the invaders out of the country. But this prince was not on the horizon: Cesare Borgia, his false incarnation, had just met a miserable end, and his friend Machiavelli was banned and spied on as a public enemy. So the true purpose of the book had to be concealed, and the actions instrumental to that purpose became separated from it. Machiavelli's advice took on the *form* of universality: of an evil Mirror for Princes, and indeed a diabolical ethic for everyone. The universality of the *content,* its ideological relevance, soon ensued: as a prefiguration of the Enlightenment, which rationalized all things and beings into means to ends, yet at the same time, in a demonically absurd reversal, abolished all ultimate ends. *Il Principe* ultimately influenced posterity with nothing but its reputation of having severed instruments from time-honored purposes, means from moral ends—so the rising self could declare itself the only end and use all means in godless and inhuman selfishness. Worst of all, Machiavelli seemed to admit all means solely in order to sanction the most evil ones: seduction and violence.

In the center of *Il Principe* (Chapter 18) towers in fact the amazing double allegory of the prince as a fox and a lion: the bastard begot by the heraldic animals of seduction and violence. But Machiavelli's genius extended beyond any fashionable emblematizing to nasty literalness: "Necessarily, a prince must know how to act as a man and a beast." Giovanni, as man-and-beast, belongs in the unholiest of unholies of modern godlessness (however little *Il Principe* was conceived as a manual for skirt-chasers): a supporting figure in the monument for the real Machiavelli, not the one monumentalized by historical misunderstanding. The scandal of Giovanni now can be named: the proof in action that the individual achieves liberation (eliminates

God, expropriates the sovereign) by opting not alone for his rational but for his animal self. For a moment—before the Stone Guest enters—it seems as if one single person had emancipated himself for our sake, from heaven and hell alike. – Middle-class thought and morality could make some kind of peace with the blasphemy of reason, but never with the blasphemy of flesh; nor was the *summum opus* of its musical theater permitted to have the sensual animal-man as its hero. At first (with Beethoven) it cursed, then (from Hoffman to Mörike) it spiritualized, finally (with Felsenstein) it emasculated the theme, the hero. Schink's insight and courage in naming the "bestiality" of the "beast" was repressed with ever greater prudery.*

Giovanni's bestiality can be ignored by today's hypocrites because of its archaism: in willpower and splendor, he stands closer to the impiety of the Renaissance than to the cult of evil fostered by Laclos and de Sade. The modern spiritualization of seduction-and-violence finds its truth not in "infinite longing" but in perversion. The hero, however, who understands himself (like Machiavelli's "wise centaur") as animal and human, would know nothing of perversion. Where de Sade (the "post-Machiavellian") savors erotic coercion as an end in itself, Giovanni (the "Machiavellian") uses coercion to achieve his sexual aims. He may be already a victim of the bourgeois era, which has begun to denigrate his happiness and its own; but he has not yet learned to enjoy the refined novel substitutes for

---

*That Giovanni continually threatens to kill his servant is nowadays considered comical, because Leporello is so cowardly—although we saw Giovanni murder the Commendatore, who was so brave. We applaud the B-flat major aria for its vital energy—and we fail to hear how, through rhythm, tempo, color, a panicked rage pulsates under the zest of the words and the bravura of their declamation.

enjoyment. One need only consult the most virtuous author of the eighteenth century, the profane father confessor to all virgins who allowed themselves to be ravished to their soul's torment: Richardson. He invented the type of seducer who is lured by the coming victory of stolid morality into violating souls rather than bodies. Giovanni, on the contrary, was not fond of virgins; he fancied, according to Leporello, "women of all ranks, shapes, and ages." He would scarcely have understood one thought or thrill of Lovelace's; and he would rather have attempted the rape of Clarissa than have read about it, gloated and wept over it. He left such private pleasures and public cant to his critics and directors.

XXV

OVERTURE. Kierkegaard wrote about *Don Giovanni,* probably in the same year as Wagner (1841): "In the overture the music unfolds all its substance; with a few mighty wingbeats it seems to sail beyond itself, to survey the place it will glide down to." More exactly than Wagner's heavy talk about the "ideal prologue" (mistaking *Giovanni,* predicting *Lohengrin*), this metaphor describes how overtures since *Alcestis* were ultimately to measure off not the action of the opera but its span. Which are the extreme powers (ranks or ideas) in the plot: who opposes whom? – The overtures to *Le nozze di Figaro* and *Così fan tutte* do not repel but rather exemplify this design, in the negative. With shrewd artistry they weave the illusion of a single, pervading impulse, which *motu perpetuo* swallows all thematic contrasts. They announce that buffa extends into time, not space: that it knows no span, only innumerable nuances within its contiguous world.

CONCEPTS OF STYLE. Baroque or modern, space or time, domination or freedom: concepts will simplify things. They do damage to the richness of historical reality, to what once really was. But the scholarly defenders of the historical, who cram us with their endless factual details of however and nonetheless, suffocate not only thought but indeed the sensitivity to richness and detail under all their immaterial material. – To assert, as inventors of concepts do, that the past was meaningful and coherent is a crime against the past: it ignores its pain. To assert, as accusers of concepts do, that the past was meaningless and incoherent is a crime against the past: it ignores its joy and its pain. (Trying to build concepts which acknowledge remorse for their own injustice may still be the best course toward knowledge and possibly even sensibility.)

XXVII

SPACE AND TIME. Space and time: they stand for domination and freedom. But they also stand for a pure and an impure relationship in the world. Time is impure, because in it every object, every man is one thing and then an other. Thus disloyalty, betrayal become the clock of freedom, and finally the madly accelerated hourstroke of the modern age. That is perhaps the deepest theme of *Don Giovanni*.

Son and Father
On Kleist's Last Play

. . . il perdono e le grazie sono necessarie in proporzione dell' assurdità delle leggi e dell'atrocità delle condanne.

Beccaria

((

The Reconstruction of the Community

I

Suddenly and improbably the great political drama about
the Prince of Homburg emerges in 1810. There are perhaps
a dozen plays that grasp not merely some political episode,
but politics itself. The void of two thousand years that
yawns from *The Bacchae* and *Iphigenia* to *Richard II* is
matched by the innocuously shallow but epoch-wide gap
that separates Corneille's *Cinna* and *Horace* from Kleist's
Prinz Friedrich von Homburg. With their doctrines of salvation, which opened history to redemption, both the
Middle Ages and the Enlightenment excluded themselves
from that which unites the political with the tragic: an irre-
deemably closed and conclusive dialectic between the will
of the individual and the mechanism of the whole—fate. –
The enlightened dogma that the world could be totally
understood and steered by monadic reason seemed (in the
eyes of a chastened Europe) to have been taken up again,
insanely exaggerated into an agenda for global conquest,
in the life plan of Napoleon. In fact, the emperor's genius
for exploiting situations, along with his maxim that fate is
politics, had already refuted all utopian dreams of Reason,
and by Jena at the latest had swept them into the rubbish.
Thus ended a long period of nonpolitics (pretended "supra-

politics"), which had been decreed by absolutism, exploited by the Enlightenment, and realized in the Reign of Terror. It was Napoleon, the enemy and teacher, who helped his young mortal foe to conceive of a tragedy that dealt no longer with psychological projections clothed in knights' armor and amazons' veils, but with Prussia and Heinrich von Kleist.

Kleist's immense effort to recoup the political—and his lethally trenchant dramatization of it—can be measured by the distance between the play and its source. The anecdote of the cavalry general's disobedience and the Grand Elector's mercy on June 28, 1675, was first fabricated in 1748 by Friedrich II for his *Histoire de la Maison de Brandenbourg.* Kleist rediscovered the oft-cited moral lesson in the army chaplain K. H. Krause's *Patriotic Reader,* which he borrowed for two months from the Dresden Library in 1809. Krause's account of the victory celebration after the battle of Fehrbellin calls for close comparison with Kleist's astounding scenes 9 and 10 in Act II: "The Prince Friedrich von Hessenhomburg, *conscious of his lapse in service,* stood at some distance and did not dare to raise his glance to the severely righteous ruler. The Elector *kindly beckoned* for him to approach: 'If,' he said, 'I wished to treat you as the severity of martial law dictates, you would deserve death. But may God preserve me from tainting my hands with the blood of a man who has been a prime instrument of my victory.' With a *fatherly admonition* to be more careful in the future, *he embraced him* and assured him of all his esteem and friendship."

What happens in Kleist, then, does not happen in his source. Indeed, the characters agree to act as if nothing had happened. It is the same in Friedrich the Great: the Elector's mercy forestalls his verdict so impatiently that the verdict, and therefore the mercy, never really comes to pass. As an author, Friedrich shared the enlightened taste for rationalizing away recalcitrant experience. His historical forgery propounds the ruler's "kindness," his *clemenza,* as that fear of conflict and impotence in punishing which the propaganda of late absolutism (less deceptive than self-deceiving) exalted to an ideal. Kleist, however, implacably drove all the admonitory pragmatism out of his material and replaced its benign moralizing dullness with the sharpest political edge. Krause's scene, replete with kind beckoning, fits with the honest general who trustily admits his guilt; Kleist's scene, with its suffocating rigidity, clashes with the young hero's crazed jubilation at his victory. The two scenes seem distortions of each other, horribly grotesque parodies. Their contrast helps us to sense the horror under the often graceful infallibility in Kleist's structures of language and scene. Spasms of fear—the freezing and stumbling of speech and action are the price of his immense venture (as if it had to stop and restart, again and again, on the verge of nothingness): his attempt to construct the state anew in view of the individual, and the individual in view of the state.

2

And yet Kleist's *novissimum* does not strike us at first with its novelty. Images of the most ancient political experience stream into it, filling its cells of thought and action: as if all past knowledge of power, conflict, atonement, now suddenly revived, had only been waiting for the era of utopian self-deception to end. The plot of the *Prinz von Homburg,* singular as it seems, has absorbed myths from the great tragedies of the Ancients and the Baroque—not as tried-and-true, threadbare stage stratagems, but as substrata of a long-repressed memory of the race, which now reasserts itself against a neatly preordained universal history. Kleist's dramatic conflict moves within the two pairs of concepts that have long been used to grasp the essence of the state and the aspiration of the individual in it: the now bloody, now healing struggle-and-appeasement systems of *law and mercy* and of *individuation and self-sacrifice*. The first, seemingly more archaic pair of opposites was not fully established until the French Baroque (being bound to absolutism, sovereignty); the second, deceptively more modern pair had already appeared in ancient Athens (unbound by democracy, autonomy). Their purest literary prototypes are Corneille's *Cinna* with its breakthrough to mercy, and Euripides' *Iphigenia at Aulis* with its apotheosis of sacrifice. But the *Prinz von Homburg* is the first and perhaps the only tragedy to compress into one those two models so contrary in intent and origin. Their union is enforced under the history-shaping, life-threatening pressure of the demand to fit the new, infinite human subject into the (post-enlightened, post-revolutionary) alien finitude of the world.

Both the Periclean Greek and the Frenchman of the *grand siècle* would have laughed at the notion that the self was infinite, whereas reality was finite. But it is precisely this foolhardy inversion that gives the *Homburg* tale its tragic premise and almost farcical sub-premise—as if the fate of the modern era were modeled on the joke of the elephant and the mouse. Kleist learned to believe in the incommensurability of the individual in his Rousseauistic youth, to suffer and comprehend it in his Kant crisis, and to express it with *Penthesilea*. The Prince's every syllable bespeaks and bewails it with an embarrassing, unavoidable immediacy. This is why the play is hard to bear: all the reality of the ego, attested by speech and speechlessness, obtruding on us with its trances and sufferings, is to be stamped out by the suprareal, unreal force of the law. – Therefore, tradition is burdened with a most difficult task for the *Prinz von Homburg*. Kleist sets those two well-tested conceptual machines toward each other not only to resurrect the oldest political experience, but even more to heal the most recent rupture between the world of the subject and the world of the object. With acute ingenuity, or wishful thinking, he claims that the two political processes are one process of life: that the dynamic definition of the state through law leading to mercy, and of the self through individuation leading to self-sacrifice, complement one another organically—that is, orgastically. In mercy the state shall embrace the incommensurability of the individual; in self-sacrifice the individual shall pour himself forth into the universality of the state.

The two processes indeed do harbor something seductively complementary. On the one hand, political theory has always suspected that law without mercy remains but retribution—the codified perpetuity of revenge, which stabilizes the world in the condition of lethal violence. Mercy (if it does not spring from mere whim or weakness) brings about a better law, the true birth of the state. On the other hand, ethics declares that individuation without self-sacrifice will deteriorate into anarchic egoism, which destroys itself in the war of everyone against everyone. Self-sacrifice (if it is dictated not by dumb obedience but by the recognition of the universal in oneself) brings true individuation and the advent of the citizen of the *polis*. These two dialectical moves become shockingly concrete in the two main actions of the *Homburg* drama, in the uncertain but fixed steps of the Elector and the Prince. It is the emotional and cognitive fullness of this double progress that abnegates the source of the play: Friedrich's (in truth, Metastasio's) precious ballet of amnesty and contri-tion, that beckoning, embracing pas-de-deux of sovereign and subordinate in their contest of selflessness. – Mercy, to which Kleist's Elector fights his way clear, is neither sentimental extenuation nor permissive custom-tailoring of laws and punishments, and even less their authority-avoiding revocation. At the conclusion of a frenzied, mute struggle of minds and powers, mercy shines out as the founding of a state that is built on law but inhabited by spontaneity: the "fatherland." In turn, the self-sacrifice that Kleist's Prince flees, seeks, accepts in wild *peripeteias* will not fade into a tapestry-ready genuflection of high-minded repentance; it finds fulfillment as the secluded ego's transfiguration through torturous trial into a complete self, capable of community. The double action of the *Prinz von Homburg,* in the moment when it seems to succeed, grows into the promise of real, or at least possible, union. It pledges the reconstruction of the community, without betraying the sensibility of the subject, the rise of the modern experience.

126

3

But if Kleist's imagination and realism live in the unprecedented, pulsating and trembling concreteness of two processes of thought turned action, then they culminate in the obstacles of that twofold action, reconciliation. Between law and mercy the Elector's *fear of anarchy* interposes, forcing him to cling stubbornly to retribution. Natalie soothes him in vain: "Oh, Sire! Why this concern? The Fatherland? / It shall not, just because you're moved to mercy, / Crumble to dust and perish." – Between individuation and self-sacrifice the Prince's *fear of death* is wedged, throwing him ("helpless, abandoned") back on his narrowest, most confused ego. Amidst the crushing actuality of fear, Natalie's conjuration in the conditional, trying once more to mediate, sounds strangely pedantic, ineffective: "But if the Elector cannot change the law's / Commandment, if he *cannot!* then you shall, / A brave man, submit bravely to his verdict." She herself knows better—and echoes the coward's cry for help, driving an abrupt caesura into the blank verse: "He thinks of nothing but this one thing: rescue!" Kleist's thematic invention, the tale of hard-won, or hopeless, reconciliation between the infinite subject and finite reality, finds its correlative in Kleist's psychological discovery: fear as the vanishing-point of characterization. To Kleist, character no longer means the unified source and form of energy that the visible and active individual brings to the community; it rather means the disunion, specific to each individual, between the substance which he knows himself to be and the shape in which he is painfully forced to appear to others and act on others. Fear therefore restlessly patrols the borderline, the gap between the sense of self and the world of appearance. More succinctly, that is, dramatically: fear is the individual's intuition that he is about to fall from the universal. Thus fear is the true location of his uniqueness.

That the singular core of each character lies in his fear puts us at the heart of the dilemma in *Prinz Friedrich von Homburg*. The more artfully and persuasively Kleist portrays the uniqueness-as-isolation of his characters, the more involuntarily and fatally he must admit that they refuse to integrate into the totality of the plot. But it is precisely the integration of the characters' inmost experience into the story's public meaning that decides the success or failure of not only the artistic effort but also the political message in *Homburg*. Kleist's life was periodically infected and ravaged by the reopening of the scar between the world of the subject and of the object; his wooing met with dismayed refusal, his plans provoked misunderstanding. This structure recurs in his work: the details work against the design, and the utmost truth of the conflicts impugns the credibility of their resolution. – In opposition to the mendacious concord that German romanticism, patriotism, imperialism are to extort from the individual, Kleist (while his conciliatory construct founders on the irrefutable experience of the ego) predicts a crisis of violent discord. It will alter not only the valuation of individuality but also the legitimation of the state. The more concrete and yet boundless that the ego perceives itself, the more abstractly and yet brutally will authority confront it. In drama: *Cinna* demanded a specific choice between a monarchy and a republic; in the *Prinz von Homburg,* command opposes *all* disobedience. In history: Baroque sovereignty was obliged to recognize even the rebel as a political opponent (a holdover from the civil war that it claimed to have ended); the new regime takes the individual as such to be its enemy—an eternal and daily threat, a mess of insubordination.* The borderline character Everyman used to be called a conspirator; now he is called a terrorist. Taming him requires not monarchic but total power. *Homburg* arouses and dramatizes this tendency—but it avoids, lest all viable dramatic form be demolished, its utmost consequence.

In August or September 1809 Kleist wrote a manifesto

* Such abstract and coarse exacerbation of conflicts forces the crisis of *Homburg.* How senseless it would have seemed to the Greeks (on stage and in the audience), if the west wind had suddenly begun to blow, to send Iphigenia nonetheless to the sacrificial altar; and how eagerly Augustus would have rewarded Cinna instead of punishing him, if his revolt had aimed at the emperor's victory instead of his ruin. In *Homburg,* such (humane) pragmatism is ignored. The fatherland is saved, the prince is proved its devoted subject, indeed its hero; nonetheless he must die.

On the Rescue of Austria. It challenges the Hapsburg emperor to act as "reconstructor and provisory regent of the Germans" and seize power over the whole of Germany, unlimited by any constitution. Scholars have sensibly dated the Austria manuscript as contemporary with *Prinz Friedrich von Homburg*—and absurdly mixed up the two. Richard Samuel speculates that both works "integrate authority with a 'democratic' bias." The manifesto, however, begins: "Any all-encompassing danger, if it be met appropriately, gives the state a *momentary* democratic *appearance*." Kleist propagandizes the appeal to the people as a reluctantly used and deceptive provisional measure (demagogy, not democracy) for enforcing the essentially provisional: the state of emergency, dictatorship. "The government is authorized to make . . . every specific demand on the people, to use their strength arbitrarily in every conceivable way, and to bring about respect for the spirit of its orders, so that they will be obeyed." – Kleist's formula for dictatorship refers to the early Roman mandate for a supreme command (unrestricted but temporary) in time of war—yet his language and ethics anticipate the seizure of power over a modern society by a totalitarian mafia. His ideas, instructions for action, scarcely conceal a postrevolutionary scorn for the moribund monarchy. The transfer of legitimation from monarchy to dictatorship, which the would-be publicist recommends to the ruler, apes and surpasses Napoleon's Caesarism, which it pretends to oppose. The Hapsburg ruler acted contrary to the unsought advice: he definitely waived claim to the title of Holy Roman emperor (which in fact was no longer good for anything except perhaps a dictatorship) and withdrew to his hereditary legitimacy in Austria. Afer Kleist had killed himself and Napoleon had done himself in with conquests, Europe was given a last, poorly exploited opportunity: it was spared totalitarian theory, of the right or left, for another thirty years, and totalitarian practice for more than a century.

To collate the *Prinz von Homburg* with Kleist's political program of 1808–1809 (from the dramatist's assault *Hermannsschlacht* to the journalist's propaganda *Rescue of Austria*) is rewarding indeed—not because the problems they attack are identical, but because the solutions they plead for are so glaringly different. Those ill-fated manifestos use the pretext of an urgent national emergency to anticipate the modern breakdown of all mediations, humanizations—until the scorn for petty old princelings erupts in a call for new total power. The tragedy with a happy end, on the contrary, tries to halt the very dissociation of individual and community that it portrays. It seeks to extricate itself from the feud between subjective chaos and institutional terror and find rescue, for one last time, under the wing of patriarchy. No one longed with such fervent despair and hope for a fatherly gentle mediation as did the poet who had experienced and spelled out the failure of mediation. If the European Restoration had been less cowardly, and Kleist less bold, it would have hailed the *Prinz von Homburg* as its credo *(quia absurdum)*.

((((

The Deceit of Tradition

I

Old Prussia, a small, manageable country, is the home of
patriarchy in *Prinz Friedrich von Homburg*. The antagonists
compete in reminding one another of its time-honored
heritage. The Elector discreetly harps on it when he exacts
self-sacrificial discipline from the younger man; but the
Prince claims the literal existence of "a German heart of
the good ancient mettle" when he demands from the older
man "generosity and love," amnesty. The images of *po-
liteia* that arise here, gently shimmering, depict a warm,
parochial world of closeness and mutual faith, endangered
by two evils: the rigid denominations of law and the name-
less chaos of anarchy. Kleist's love was true to a wished-
for Prussia; his hatred and dread were reserved for the
"Roman" spirit, which, long before the assault of Napoleon, had overwhelmed the young provincial in the me-
tropolis of Paris: the depersonalized, nonpaternal grand
machine of centralism vis-à-vis a blindly surging mass of
isolated, fatherless individuals. The shock of Paris marked
the axis of symmetry for his decisive year of 1801: before
it, he was deserted by his friend, suffered the Kant crisis,
and fled from civil service; after it, he tried to live as a poet
and peasant, first envisioned *Schroffenstein,* and jilted his

fiancée. Kleist returned from the "abominable place" not as a legitimist, but as an ardent proponent of patriarchy. The vulnerable restorative idyll of his *Prinz von Homburg* takes its form and beauty from a hoped-for, suffered-for declaration of peace between father and son. But even in his raging diatribe *A German Catechism,* there is magic when son and father, clumsy, cosy, huddle together before the flaming panorama of the world, where the patriarchal family and the fatherland are being strangled by Napoleon, "the patricidal spirit from hell."

The *Prinz von Homburg* glorifies Friedrich Wilhelm I as the *patrem patriae.* In 1809, Kleist's closest political friend Adam Müller had advised Prussian poets to make a backward leap (over the corpse of the childless, antipaternal Friedrich II) to the "much more national" Grand Elector. Kleist was the very first to follow this advice. But his model son's eagerness is distorted by the mirror of his life into penitence for his humiliating, compulsively repeated failure to prove himself a man (a potential father) in the eyes of his family and country. – Heinrich von Kleist, descended from a line of military officers, had lost his father at the age of eleven. He conceived himself, indeed chose himself, not as a fatherless free man but as an abandoned, that is, rejected, son. At the age of twenty-two he tried to throw off the paternal heritage, resigning his commission. He still wanted to justify himself (in a moving, youthfully stubborn letter to his teacher Martini): "For me, the greatest miracles of military discipline, the object of every connoisseur's astonishment, became the object of hearty contempt; I considered officers as so many drill-masters, the soldiers as so many slaves, and when the whole regiment did its tricks, to me it seemed a living monument of tyranny." But his will to liberation was soon to change into feelings of guilt, as attested by the very next sentence, which already betrays a secret of the *Homburg* psychology: "I was often forced to punish where I would have liked to pardon, or I pardoned where I should have punished, and *in both cases I felt I myself deserved punishment.*" Not insubordination per se damned Homburg/Kleist to stay forever a guilty son—but the fact that from every attempt at rebellion he learned only his incompetence in the father's role: in punishing and pardoning, laying down laws and granting mercy.

The drama is about patriarchy—for Kleist, about the guilt of the (real) son toward the (imagined) father. In 1675 Friedrich Wilhelm had half-a-dozen sons, the heir to the throne was eighteen years old, and the Prince of Hessen-Homburg was forty-two. If the historical, history-concocting anecdote of the Elector and the Prince was to be molded into a play about the perfect patriarchy, then the Elector's sons had to disappear. Kleist arranged the dynastic massacre, but the responsibility for it falls on his hero. It works as an undercurrent throughout the play: as if Homburg, another Gloucester, had disposed of his rightfully entitled nephews. To stress the effect, it is slyly intimated that Natalie is a kind of successor to the throne. The sleepwalking Prince's words to her—"My beloved! My bride!"—elicit a mysterious dread in the courtiers, which is heightened and explained when he addresses the Elector as "My father!" Homburg's role as lover is evidently but a disguise for his pretending to the role of son, which makes him primordially guilty of usurpation. – Why wanting to be a son is a crime is clarified when Homburg woos Natalie after the battle. Only the Elector's presumed death (effected by fear and desire, as in a nightmare) gives the Prince a right to his distant relative's niece, or "little daughter." His victory through disobedience is patricide: not just because it seems to have led to the Elector's death, but because it reveals and seemingly realizes the Prince's wish to replace the Elector. To the "orphaned girl" he calls out: "I, Lady, will assume your cause!" In utter hypocrisy or blindness he concludes the scene of his triumph with a prayer to his murdered rival: "Would that we / Could stammer: Father, give us now your blessing!" From above comes no blessing, but a curse.

At the moment when the ruler/father is put aside and canonized, the fate of the pretender/son turns from ascent to decline. The break is instantly expressed by terms of kinship. When the young man sees the old man who he hoped was dead walk toward him in vengeance, he refuses for the first and only time to be called "son." "My *cousin* Friedrich yearns to play old Brutus . . . / He shall, by God, not find in me the son." He knows that to be a son would be to die for the unsuccessful patricide. And yet not to be a son soon seems to him worse than death. He offers his own death in order to buy back his father: "To you, my sovereign, *whom I used to call / A sweeter name,* now cast away in folly, / To you I come to kneel, deeply contrite! . . . / Now death will wash me clean of all my guilt." And now indeed, for the first and only time, the Elector calls the Prince "my son." He "kisses his forehead." The father seems to recognize his son only by the act of filial self-sacrifice.

2

Thus the *Prinz von Homburg* takes its place in the millennia-long series of myths, tragedies, oratorios, operas concerned with children's sacrifice and self-sacrifice. Their structure traps the father between godfearing piety (or official duty) and parental love. Political theory exalted his keenest anguish to a paradigm in the story of Brutus the Elder; and theology, by appointing Isaac a precursor of Christ, turned even God the Father into a follower of Abraham the Patriarch. Because the tied-together tales of Abraham, Jephthah, Agamemnon, Idomeneus are always told from the father's perspective, never the child's, they bestow on the fathers divine praise and public gratitude. But the tied-up child (Abraham "bound Isaac his son, and laid him on the altar upon the wood") receives only instrumental sanctification as he perishes. The stubborn repetition in world history of this deed and its recompense, with the same kind of celebration invariably following after the same kind of suffering, leads us to suspect that such an act of faith and grief, pleasing to God and the tribe, is in truth only a ritualized euphemism for the generations' eternally murderous struggle for power. – Kleist's desperate, unconditional search for community arrived at the dire intuition that the killing of a son may be not the exception but the very rule in patriarchy. Hence the *Homburg* experiment of fusing the models of *Cinna* and *Iphigenia* makes new, terrible sense. The guiltless girl whose self-sacrifice brought the promise of emancipation is replaced with the guilt-ridden son whose rebellion will come to justify the state's frequent relapses into barbarity. Tradition from now on threatens to bring to modern times the message of interminable destruction, not of possible salvation.

Fathers who drag their *daughters* to the sacrificial altar, however, will continue to be entitled to the Agamemnon bonus: the spectator is ready to believe that the murderer nonetheless hates to murder. Because no one can suspect the daughter-killers of using a pious pretext to do away with their successors, their tales obscure the politico-theological question of patriarchy—turning it into a pleasurable exercise of empathy with sublimely divided and spectacularly gripping sentiments. The daughter's guiltless death rubs off on the father as pure innocence, for tragedy excludes pure crime. Yet the great tragedians (and psychologists) Euripides and Racine had enough courage to hint at the callous sophistry of such a sentimental and conventional response. They show Agamemnon not only in the heroic collision between paternal and civic duty but also in the twilight of cowardice and ambition, while they resoundingly celebrate Iphigenia.* – A perplexing reversal is initiated by Diderot, in a letter to Sophie Volland of November 6, 1760. With the admiration of a connoisseur and the wink of an accomplice, he praises the tricks ("cette boîte") he asserts that Racine was using—not just to exculpate the king, but to make him the focus of every spectator's empathy. Diderot's Agamemnon clears the way for Lessing's Odoardo. At the dawn of the new, bourgeois repression, the paterfamilias is seen as the true hero of tragedy; and a docile new public is being taught (as was the coarsest ancient audience) that the father who sacrifices his child suffers more, deserves more compassion than the child who is sacrificed.

In interrogating *Homburg,* the mythical riddles of its

---

*But even to glorify the self-immolating girl conduces to distract us from the shame of the father who does not prevent her immolation. Brutalized by training in Jansenist self-denial, the commentary on Jephthah in the *Bible de Royaumont* (1670) expressly hails this side effect: "Even if the father's behavior deserves censure, the daughter's earns all our admiration . . . She repairs somehow what may have been wrong [*défectueux*] on her father's part. She turns an impious slaughter into a God-pleasing sacrifice." Not until the early Enlightenment did commentators denounce the scandal of forcing the girl, nearly murdered, to exculpate her murderer. With privatist, antipolitical morality, Saint-Evremond assails the unnatural act of Agamemnon, who not only tolerates but officiates at Iphigenia's death.

context help us clarify the historical meaning of its text. The play's appeal to tradition, its yearning for and despair about patriarchy, its reawakening of politics—all this required, in 1810, a radical change in drama's basic conflict and thus in its subject matter. Kleist's father-and-son tragedy assailed the forty-year-long fashion of sentimental father-and-daughter plays, swollen with the ideology of nature, equated with family. He rebutted a petty bourgeois dramaturgy which unmasked or slandered paternal authority of the superior classes, but sentimentalized and moralized paternal oppression within its own class. Whereas the *drame bourgeois,* with tearful eyes and smacking lips, perverted all virgin daughters (from Lessing's Emilia to Sade's Ernestine) into the embodiment of suffering innocence, Kleist's Prince, crushed by guilt, throws himself at the feet of the archaic princess: worshipping her not as the one who had innocently suffered, but as the primeval rescuer rescued. The Prince's helplessly wild *peripeteias,* of fear (III, 5) and self-sacrifice (V, 7), look to Euripides' lines (as adapted in 1789 by Schiller):

Iphigenia: Don't kill me in full flower!—Look, the sun
Is so dear! Do not force me before my time
To see what lies below! . . .
Who wishes his own death is mad! *It's better
To live in shame than die admired!*

Homburg: O mother, God's world is so beautiful!
I beg you, do not make me go before
My hour has struck to those black shades
   below . . .
Since I have seen my grave *I care for nothing
Except to live—in honor or without.*

It is not in this deepest distress of "better to live in shame than die admired" that Homburg's alliance with Iphigenia breaks down, but in the constraint to identify with affirmative values:

Iphigenia: Now listen to the outcome of my soul's
             Most calm consideration! *I am resolved*
             To die—but not against my will,
             Of my own choice to honorably die! . . .
             I will have saved Greece . . .

Homburg: Thus I have thought the matter out, and now
             I wish to die *the death decreed* for me! . . .
             Quiet! It is my absolute desire!
             I'll glorify the sacred law of war,
             Broken by me before the entire army,
             With voluntary death.

With pious love for life, Iphigenia immolates herself for Greece; intoxicated by death, Homburg kills himself for martial law. She wants victory over the barbarians; he yearns to "triumph" over "the enemy *in us,* license and defiance." The virgin chooses a heroic death, the hero a death for discipline.

At the Kleistian crossroads of law leading to mercy and individuation leading to self-sacrifice, no reconciliation with the whole awaits the subject. Rather, the elements of a possible society are dissociated and maliciously at war. Law seizes on self-sacrifice, as if that offering were due only to it, to reinforcing and solidifying its worldwide rule. The true goal of Euripides' sacrificial procession, individuation, is forced out of the play—crushed by the Elector's martial law, which demands to rule in the Prince's soul as well. From now on, the defeated, penitent individual must see the rise of the subject as what the universal has always suspected it to be: "license" and "defiance."

3

Mercy has, finally, the most unrewarding part in *Prinz Friedrich von Homburg,* the last *clemenza* play in the great European tradition. She seems quite alien, an outcast in a realm where the subordinate's cry for rescue is met only with bafflement, as a disgraceful aberration: "It cannot really be!? He begs for mercy?" But the true aberration, true disgrace of *Homburg* is not the Prince's oft-reviled fear of death (which caused the play to be banned in Berlin until 1828, and then, after the third performance, "forever"), but the much-glorified answer to it: the Elector's letter of mercy. What even Montesquieu, the shrewdest enemy of absolutism, referred to as "the most beautiful attribute of sovereignty, the gift of mercy"—this gift is refashioned by the sovereign himself into a trap. – For the Elector's "He is pardoned" in the middle of the play proves to be a lie. His letter does not only avoid canceling the subordinate's guilt by the ruler's prerogative; rather, the Prince's guilt is spitefully, deceptively sealed by the Elector's very concession. While the message of the letter pretends to turn the culprit into his own dispenser of mercy, its wording in fact turns him into his own court of appeal: "If he can *claim* the verdict is unjust, / Then it shall be annulled: and he is free." Thus, the theologico-political place of mercy is occupied, and the miraculous fissure for supreme forgiveness filled up, by precisely that which mercy is meant to break through: the totality of judgment. "And he is free"? In the

Prince's reply, if only we are prepared to hear it, Kleist has encoded all the helpless lack of freedom of the individual trapped in a dungeon universe of total judgment: "That he is *unjust,* as is his condition, / I *cannot* write him that; if you *constrain* me . . ." The subject must decide his freedom in the midst of labyrinthine constraints. Even worse: he will decide to see such constraint as his freedom. He will carry out, as a subject, what is being carried out upon him, the liquidation of the subject.

Critics have tried to read bitterness toward the Prussian *Rechtsstaat* into the play. Before Kleist was born, Beccaria's and Voltaire's campaign for justice had flooded Europe. Meanwhile the German princes, Friedrich most successfully, were able to link their pact with the commoners to legality rather than justice. The monarch won admiration not by canceling bad laws but by observing his own laws. The German climate of repressive respectability came into being. There, the subordinate does not fight for his (and everyone else's) rights but makes sure that none of his neighbors gets more of them than he does. – Kleist's critique of Prussia, however, is not directed against this abortion of *aequitas*. Here too he seeks his own version of the modern by regressing beyond the Enlightenment: he demands from the ruler generosity instead of a constitution and a code, from the state more spontaneity instead of more rationality. Again, he provocatively sharpens the mechanism of his dramatic plot almost beyond bearing; it is to rake up all the extenuating circumstances known to enlightened jurisprudence, only to sweep them all aside. Anything that could ever warrant or call for pardon before the court of reason speaks for the Prince: his lack of intention or consciousness of wrongdoing, his personal merit, the benefit rather than the harm of his deed to the community—even his impaired competence before the battle (from sleepwalking in the night and recalling it in the morning). Yet all rationalistic quibbling is deflected by the Elector's silence. Amnesty is not meant to resolve guilt into motives; instead, unfounded, unfathomable mercy simply descends upon the guilty. The Elector's silence, however, separates his decision not only from a polemically misinterpreted Enlightenment, but also from its own chosen tradition in the Baroque. For to disdain the rhetorical self-revelation of clemency also cancels its solemn public act (the command to "Rise!" turned into a gesture), which wondrously united sparing with renewing, preservation with creation. The *Prinz von Homburg* is a prophecy of the European Restoration—above all because it shows that the opportunity soon after 1810 to create from the healed past a future (a community) will be forfeited in advance.

When at the end of the last, belated *clemenza* drama, mercy at long last makes its belated entrance, its true object has long been extinguished. Once, in barbarian or even feudal times, the deed of arbitrary pardon might have applied just to the bare life or the abstract honor of a guilty (defeated) man. At the beginning of the modern age even those with power sense reluctantly that mercy now must aim at something deeply different. The field marshal, mired in his Baroque bureaucrat's jargon, trembling with rage and dread, slanders that target as "rebellion"; the Elector, with a view to totalitarian options, scolds it as "disorder." The terminology of both is destructively misdirected; within mercy's new domain, it focuses on not what should be rescued but what must obsessively be feared and annihilated: the enemy. – This hostility, stemming from both the Baroque and the modern era, defined, encircled, and crushed the ephemeral being that sought to escape from patriarchy's disastrous progress from the absolute to the total state. For it happened that during Europe's grace period between sovereignty and dictatorship a new entity truly in need of mercy arose—to be exterminated in Kleist's drama, with Kleist himself. Its rightful name was: the uniqueness of the subject, the aspiration of sons, *autonomy*. – Because the *Prinz von Homburg* could not be helped by tradition, we are permitted, indeed compelled to reverse the question: How does tradition appear in the cataclysmal light of Kleist's most sublime and beautiful failure? Did his adventurous experiment in reconciliation-as-community fail because of his own "hypochondria" (which Goethe inexorably censured), because of the subjectivist Fall of the modern mind? Or rather did the lies of former reconciliations (which always had justified the father/totality and paid off the son/subject with the ruler's mercy or posthumous fame) ensnare and destroy the venturer? – Further, who is to blame for the merciless terror of the state, the lawless terror of the individual, which emerged after Kleist, but whose battle he had described, whose ravages he had suffered in advance? Was the individual no longer capable of politics—or did the state grow tired of mercy, and finally also of law?

☾

Over and over, in a maniacal rage for precision, Kleist related legal trials from Basel to Fehrbellin, Huizen to Dresden, all of which hastened toward the worst possible end with apocalyptic, indeed historical, energy. History presumed to pass judgment in Kleist's own trial. It forced the breakdown of all mediation between subject and object: first by canceling the individual's rights, then by erecting total judgment, which functions the more inexorably the more it conceals, or indeed forgets, its own law. To the connoisseurs of such universal fate who made themselves Kleist's heirs (we shall be speaking of three of them), Kleist opposes the unrest of his search and struggle, the extravagance of his querulous grief. With an un-quenchable thirst for reconciliation, his oeuvre refuses to abandon the cause of the abandoned individual. Because he did not entrust his cause to the judgment of history but kept fighting for it with each line of his plays and stories, perfected in pain, his trial still continues beyond the juris-diction of reality—ever since that first, most unjust judg-ment that he passed on himself: ending his life after the *Prinz von Homburg* was finished.

《 《 《

Fear and Trembling: A Postscript

Kierkegaard's hero is silent—the primeval father, the patriarch Abraham. "Abraham cannot be mediated, and the same thing can be expressed also by saying that he cannot talk." Yet if Abraham (loading his donkey one early morning with kindling and wood, knife and child) suddenly wanted to say what he knew in his heart about God, himself, and Isaac—then his tongue would beget, his mouth would bring forth that most Kleistian of discourses: words that cause a misunderstanding. "So soon as I talk I express the universal; and if I do not so, no one can understand me." This logic of the unspeakable from 1843 pushes the tragedy about the failure of speech from 1810 to its purest, final consequence: the collapse of all mediation. The *Prinz von Homburg* ends up in *Fear and Trembling*. – Kleist was still attempting, in doubt and despair, to delay the individual's fall into his own infinity. Kierkegaard however builds his castle of the new theology on the very abyss that splits the individual from the universal. "Faith is precisely this paradox, that the individual as the particular is higher than the universal, is justified over against it, is not subordinate but superior . . . that the individual as the particular stands in an absolute relation to the absolute." What a reversal in time of need: God himself spares us the drudgery of reconciling the painfully rebellious individual with the community. Blessings rather than curses from on high are bestowed on the incommensurable, solitary subject. Kleist's defeat becomes Kierkegaard's triumph.

But however much the patriarch squirms free of the universal, however much he soars to the level of the absolute, he is still forced to commit the sacrifice. He immolates himself by immolating his flesh and blood, his "only son" as God rightly phrases it (for he has already chased his first son into the wilderness). The "absolute relation" chooses to owe its origin and authority not to the new freedom of the self, but to a pact between fathers, the oldest of Covenants. Still, its idiom evokes archaic piety less than up-to-date dictatorship: orders and silence. This is what Kierkegaard silently passes over, that Abraham's silence toward Isaac on the long journey to Mount Moriah cruelly, servilely imitates God's silence toward Abraham; and that the suffering subjectivity of his relation of faith ultimately only reproduces, enacts, and glorifies the matter-of-fact brutality of this relationship between command and obedience. – Kierkegaard's achievement, the depoliticization of ethics, has a radically political result. Within the preserve of private authenticity, the figure of the father (changing from the Elector to the patriarch) switches from the rule of law back to the violence of myth. In that same preserve, the self-serving pretense of superannuated tragic kings—that the impotent love of the parent must unfortunately yield to the omnipotent duty of the ruler—can change undisturbed into practical advice for future despots: that the voluntary disempowerment of the individual will best further the limitless empowerment of one single person, the totalitarian outcome of patriarchy. This is what Abraham's silence says: the commandment to sacrifice that comes from above, from the father to the father against the son, shall no longer be questioned either by the sacrificer or by the victim, but must be obeyed in fear and trembling. The absolute is the silent universal. It is sheer domination, which scorns even to justify its license to kill.

The chapter on the defeated experiment of autonomy, written by the new (and yet always the same) patriarchy, ends with the dissolution of the public sphere. Kierkegaard's praise-and-destruction of *Don Giovanni* (1841–1842) never mentions the ensemble. He erases any memory of the open space of autonomy created by free individuals, who could open their minds and hearts to one another: the moment is forgotten when every emotion became speech, all speech became action. Kierkegaard's praise-and-restoration of the Abraham legend (1843) submerges the speech of his hero in a tortured interior monologue, above which emotion and action join in a mute neo-barbaric alliance, for the purpose of death-dealing if necessary. Meanwhile, the author of the speechless hero made tortured speech (full of the bad jokes of a man whose joys have all been tainted) into his style, indeed into the exemplary genre of his oeuvre: the self-advertisement— announcement and denunciation—of that remainder of individuality that had not yet turned to silence. – After Kierkegaard, the disabled self survives the annihilation of the autonomous subject, which it announces, by excepting itself (as a political theologian or mythologist) from the common fate: to be the self-appointed spokesman of mute domination. It prophesies, propagates a new world of sacrifice, whose murderous law is impenetrability— and whose murderous impenetrability will be called law. Soon, Franz Kafka's tales and Carl Schmitt's jurisprudence will mock the enlightened demand for clear and accessible laws as liberal hairsplitting; indeed such querulous claim of the individual will constitute, for the court of mythical willfulness, proof of his guilt, the very reason for his condemnation. In "The Judgment" ("Das Urteil," 1912), the legal exegete of poets shapes the irreducible decision from above into his verdict: the execution of the son by the father. In *Law and Judgment* (*Gesetz und Urteil,* 1912), the allegorist of legal theoreticians formalizes the undeducible decision of a judge into the method of all judgment: into the disenfranchisement, disempowerment, and finally obliteration of the always guilty individual.*

When later a lawless and merciless government simply equates its law with the obliteration of the powerless, that jurist will justify the barefaced murders by the empowered *Führer,* calling them "die richterlich rächende Verwirklichung dieses Rechts"—"the avenging judicial realization of this law" (Carl Schmitt, *Der Führer schützt das Recht,* 1934). The play on words, passed off as an etymological return to roots, aspires to oracular ambiguity and malice: it plunges law *(Recht)* back into its alleged origin in vengeance *(Rache).* After two and a half millennia the Erinyes cast off their masks of the Eumenides. The vengeful furies extort from patriarchy, which once tamed their immemorial rule with law, the price for its new, untamed rule: the relapse of law into total, murderous revenge.

---

*Kafka's and Schmitt's subsequent works also display disconcerting parallels of time and theme. Kafka's *In the Penal Colony* and *The Trial* and Schmitt's *The Value of the State and the Worth of the Individual* were written in 1914; Kafka's *The Castle* and Schmitt's *Dictatorship* and *Political Theology* between 1920 and 1922. We must not overlook the moral difference between the one who was existentially suffering and the one who was intellectually enjoying and politically exploiting the process that both of them foresaw and described. Yet extremism of perception (utmost rational clarity in predicting the fall of reason) singularly connects not only the insight but also the style of the two contemporaries.

⟨

NICHTS IST SO HÄSSLICH ALS DIE RACHE. "Nothing is so hateful as revenge": the concluding vaudeville of *Die Entführung aus dem Serail* teaches us this at the moment (bathed in ironically fairytale stage light, glad daybreak's light) when Mercy first sets Autonomy free. The round sung by the liberated has the spirit and rhythm of a children's counting rhyme. The vengeful man is counted out: "Wer so viel Huld vergessen kann, / Den seh man mit Verachtung an." He "shall be scoffed at"; that is his penalty. Here, those who are counted among the supernumeraries do not find their way to prison, the madhouse, or the concentration camp. Herr Osmin has to stand in the corner until he learns what the others sing to him with gentle devotion: "to be humane, kind, and forgive unselfishly." – When Mozart decries vengeance and decrees mercy in this early-morning singspiel, he abstains (until the Pasha is left alone with his janissary puppets) from ending with a sonorous victory chorus. No priests and populace chant "Es siegte die Stärke," strength has triumphed. Rather, exultant children's voices mockingly, merrily pipe the refrain, as if the Four Boys had suddenly hidden themselves in the clothes and voices of Konstanze and Belmonte, Blonde and Pedrillo. They were asked to solve by their wits this riddle: How do we rid ourselves of evil without (out goes y-o-u!) becoming evil in the process? Why, any child knows the answer, the last refrain tells us: "If you're too dumb to understand, / You shall be scoffed at to the end."

Acknowledgments

I thank the Institute for Advanced Study in Berlin (and its director Peter Wapnewski, most heartily) for enabling me to write this book in an atmosphere of freedom and friendship. Fritz Arnold and Norbert Miller read the book in manuscript, preventing some ugly errors, and contributing to whatever may be worthwhile in it.

I.N.

I thank Margarete Kohlenbach most sincerely, and Hans-Jakob Werlen, Jay Geller, A. J. Levine, and Dorothea Frede. As always, my greatest thanks go to Stephen Hannaford.

M.F.

The publishers wish to acknowledge Howard Mayer Brown for granting permission to reprint from his edition of Jacopo Peri's *Euridice* (Madison, Wis.: A-R Editions, 1981).